the power of
crystals
and crystal healing

the power of
crystals
and crystal healing

Using the transforming power of crystals
to soothe, heal and energize

Sue Lilly and Simon Lilly

southwater

This edition is published by Southwater

Southwater is an imprint of Anness Publishing Ltd
Hermes House, 88–89 Blackfriars Road, London SE1 8HA
tel. 020 7401 2077; fax 020 7633 9499
www.southwaterbooks.com; info@anness.com

© Anness Publishing Ltd 2004, 2005

UK agent: The Manning Partnership Ltd
6 The Old Dairy, Melcombe Road, Bath BA2 3LR;
tel. 01225 478444; fax 01225 478440; sales@manning-partnership.co.uk

UK distributor: Grantham Book Services Ltd
Isaac Newton Way, Alma Park Industrial Estate, Grantham, Lincs NG31 9SD;
tel. 01476 541080; fax 01476 541061; orders@gbs.tbs-ltd.co.uk

North American agent/distributor: National Book Network
4501 Forbes Boulevard, Suite 200, Lanham, MD 20706;
tel. 301 459 3366; fax 301 429 5746; www.nbnbooks.com

Australian agent/distributor: Pan Macmillan Australia
Level 18, St Martins Tower, 31 Market St, Sydney, NSW 2000;
tel. 1300 135 113; fax 1300 135 103; customer.service@macmillan.com.au

New Zealand agent/distributor: David Bateman Ltd
30 Tarndale Grove, Off Bush Road, Albany, Auckland;
tel. (09) 415 7664; fax (09) 415 8892

A CIP catalogue record for this book is available from the British Library.

Publisher Joanna Lorenz
Managing Editor Helen Sudell
Senior Editor Joanne Rippin
Photography Michelle Garrett
Designer Nigel Partridge
Editorial Reader Jonathan Marshall
Production Controller Claire Rae

Previously published as *Crystal Healing*

10 9 8 7 6 5 4 3 2 1

This book is not intended to replace advice from a qualified medical
practitioner. Please seek a medical opinion if you have any concerns about
your health. Neither the authors nor the publishers can accept any liability for
failure to follow this advice.

Thanks to Kay Harrison of 'Evolution', Exeter and 'Crystals' of Exeter, and
also to Charlie, at Charlie's Rock Shop, London, for lending crystals and
minerals for the photography.
The publishers would like to thank the following libraries for the use of their
images: Natural History Photographic Agency: p13 top, Peter Parks; Simon
and Sue Lilly p30 bottom right.

Contents

introduction

Crystals and gemstones are a fascinating area of study, and their healing power is being increasingly recognized by complementary therapists and the general public, along with the realization that health and wellbeing are the responsibility of each individual.

Contemporary medical training is largely focused on the intricacies of the physical systems of the body and learning to recognize and treat states of disease. It often flounders where clear symptom pictures are absent. Crystal healing cannot replace the doctor's skill, but it can provide an effective series of simple techniques that can reduce stress – one of the underlying causes of many types of disease – and can help to improve our subjective, personal experience of living. Wellbeing is not simply freedom from illness, it also includes listening to our feelings, emotions and thoughts, and nurturing our spiritual lives.

Why crystals placed on or around the body should have such a profound effect on our wellbeing is still not known. However, experience is always more important than theory. Ever since humans began working with flint and living in cave shelters, we have had an intimate relationship with rock. Over hundreds of thousands of years our inbuilt instincts have revealed to us the subtle nuances that crystals and gemstones create within our own energy patterns. It takes just a little practice to reconnect with this reality.

There are thousands of minerals, each with unique crystal forms and varieties of colour. Learning to associate a crystal with the energy characteristics of its colour is an excellent way to begin to understand a stone's healing potential. This book explores the capacities of crystal healing by following the natural progression of the colour spectrum. The techniques and exercises will help you to understand the power of crystals, their capacities for healing and balancing, and how they can affect the subtle energy systems that exist within us all.

The World of Crystals

Crystals remind us of the structures upon which our universe is built. All matter, everything that is physical and solid, owes its existence to the organizing properties of crystals.

In the beginning

In all parts of the world, and from the dawn of history, crystals have been regarded as belonging to the heavens, as gifts from the spirit worlds. Their colour and brilliance have set them apart from everything else on earth. Today we know that the story of crystals is indeed the story of the creation of the universe.

Astronomers believe that after the initial expansion of the universe from its original point, clouds of hydrogen, the simplest form of matter, began to cluster together. In time, within these vast balls of hydrogen, the pressures became so great that atoms began to fuse together, releasing a huge amount of energy. These glowing spheres became the first stars. Within these stars hydrogen continued to fuse to become helium and, as the burning continued, increasingly heavy elements were formed, such as nitrogen, oxygen, carbon, iron, lead and gold.

As the first stars eventually died, some exploded sending these new elements careering throughout space where gravity created new stars and planets from them. Our own solar system and the Milky Way formed in this way. Lighter gas clouds, the remains of countless stars, were drawn towards the young sun, while the heavier elements settled into orbits further away, gradually coalescing to become the planets.

the earth

Earth formed at a distance from the sun that allowed both light and heavy elements to combine. The larger atoms sank downwards to create the planet's core of iron and nickel. The core is probably surrounded by a layer

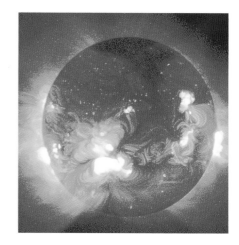

△ Every element in the universe that makes up physical matter was formed within the stars.

▽ Throughout universal space the same raw materials come together to form crystals.

△ **The apparent stability and continuity of the planet is in reality a constant cycle of erosion, deposition and metamorphosis.**

of molten metal. This layer, or mantle, around the planet comprises the greatest volume of the earth. It is 2,900km (1,800 miles) thick and composed of many layers of fluid, swirling rock. The outermost layer is the crust, a thin layer of rock that makes up the earth's continents.

The earth's crust forms less than 1 per cent of its total mass and is less than 40km (25 miles) thick over most of its surface. The distance from the surface of the planet to its centre is 6,391km (3,971 miles), yet the deepest humans have been able to drill is 8km (5 miles).

The earth's crust formed from super-heated rocks such as granite and basalt, that welled up through cracks in the surface layers either to spread out in vast domes called basoliths, or as volcanic eruptions. Rocks formed in this way are called igneous, meaning formed by fire. Millennia of erosion by wind and water wore these igneous rocks to dust. Carried downstream

by rivers, this dust was deposited at the bottom of the sea where it became compressed and eventually turned to rock again. This type of rock is called sedimentary, after the way it has been formed.

Wherever either igneous or sedimentary rock is subjected to extremes of heat or pressure by movements of the earth's crust,

its composition is altered. The change it undergoes gives it the name metamorphic rock. Crystals can be found in all types of rocks where conditions for their formation are right. As superheated gases and liquids rise to the surface, they begin to cool in the cracks and crevices of the surrounding rock, crystallizing into sparkling and coloured minerals. Harder minerals, such as diamonds and rubies, form at high temperatures in areas of volcanic activity. The crystals that form in sedimentary rock are usually much softer like gypsum and halite (common salt).

The same chemical elements appear throughout the whole of the universe. Given the right conditions, atoms of these different elements can come together to form new substances. Minerals are combinations of different elements that form the building blocks of all physical matter. All minerals, for example halite (sodium chloride – rock salt) and quartz (silicon dioxide – rock crystal), are composed of the same sorts of atoms in the same proportions.

▽ **Without the constant movement of the earth's crust many crystals would not be formed out of the sedimentary rock that lies beneath the sea.**

The nature of crystals

All minerals will form crystals, though the conditions for their growth varies from mineral to mineral. Crystals begin to grow when the right amounts of their constituent atoms are present, usually in the form of a liquid or gas, but sometimes as a solid, in conditions that allow the atoms to move into those patterns where they are in the best possible state of equilibrium with each other. Heat and pressure ensure that the atoms have the maximum movement and energy to locate these positions before conditions change.

CRYSTAL TOOLS

The first tools were made from stones such as flint and obsidian. Much later, once smelting techniques were discovered, tools and weapons were crafted from metals such as bronze and iron. Today's sophisticated technology makes use of some of the hardest elements on the planet – gemstones. Always valued as things of beauty, mystery and magic, crystals are now also prized as components in precision tools.

▽ In today's high-tech industries crystals are used in sophisticated automated tools.

structure

Once the basic pattern has been taken up by a few atoms, called the 'unit cell' of a crystal, other atoms quickly repeat the arrangement and build up the crystal lattice, the characteristic pattern of atoms unique to each mineral.

A crystal will continue to grow in this way until the exterior conditions alter or the available raw material of atoms is used up. Once formed, crystals are the most stable and organized forms of matter in the

△ These crystals are used in industry. Clockwise from top left, ruby (corundum), two pieces of tourmaline, garnet, chalcopyrite and kunzite.

universe. Their 'ideal' structure means that they often display unique qualities that make them both useful and attractive. A crystal's physical form is the expression of its interior atomic arrangement. Crystals of any given mineral always display the same relationship of symmetrical faces, and each face will meet in flat planes at the same angle. Due

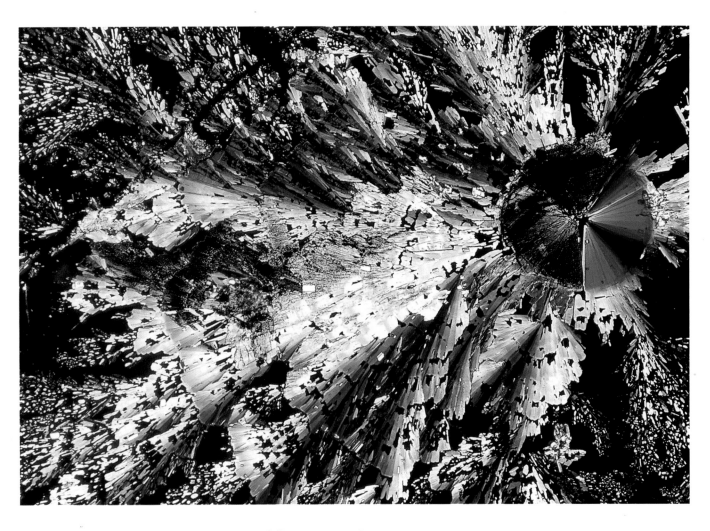

▽ Every crystal is unique in size and shape, yet all crystals of the same mineral share an identical atomic lattice structure.

to different growing circumstances no two crystals will be identical, but they will all show these characteristic features.

△ How light rays refract, reflect and move through crystal structures largely determines what colours a crystal will exhibit.

colour

Although crystals are the most perfect arrangements of matter, small imperfections are present within the lattice structure of most crystals, and in fact these anomalies are often the very things that make them so useful to us. Crystals usually get their colour from the presence of a minute amount of another substance, which distorts the lattice and deflects or alters the light rays as they pass through it. Thus quartz, which is transparent, can appear violet coloured when iron atoms are present, and pink coloured with titanium or manganese. It becomes smoky brown when the lattice is subjected to natural radiation from radioactive elements such as uranium, or intense gamma rays from space and ultraviolet radiation from the sun. Internal fractures and dislocations within the lattice can also create wonderful plays of colour and light, which make some minerals valuable as gemstones.

▽ Quartz crystal carries the properties of its elemental constituents: silicon and oxygen.

The power of crystals

Crystals are objects of beauty, fascination and mystery. They never lose their beauty so they can be treasured, hoarded and exchanged. They can become an expression of wealth. Fine examples of crystals are rare and difficult to find, which is why they have become symbols of high rank, royalty and even divinity.

magical properties

The beauty of crystals makes them a natural choice in personal adornment or the decoration of precious objects. Their uniqueness imbues them with magical power: the power to protect, to enhance, to strengthen, to uplift. They have been used as amulets to ward off harm, as talismans to encourage virtues, as magical guardians to heal, and as tools to interpret messages from the spirit world. The attraction they hold transcends time and place. Many people are keen to own their birthstone, and to discover which stone will encourage love or wealth. With the much larger range of stones from all around the world available today everyone has a favourite, and is drawn to crystals for their particular qualities of warmth, subtlety or sparkle.

▽ **Many people simply collect crystals and gemstones for their visual appeal.**

decoration and placement

Large crystal clusters are increasingly found in homes and offices. Their visual complexity and their wonderful colours make them ideal to gaze at while the mind relaxes a little. The beneficial energy that they may bring to the observer or the room they are in is an added bonus.

Crystals can be placed in the home according to feng shui, the traditional Chinese art of arranging objects, for the enhancement of positivity. The Chinese believe that they bring orderliness and clarity into life.

△ **Natural magic, in contrast to the complex rituals of ceremonial magic, has always used the unique properties of crystals.**

the spiritual healing paradigm

Crystals and gemstones have a long tradition of being used for healing. In contemporary practice there are two main ways in which they are used, both of which have parallels in much older traditions across the world. The first method can be called the 'spiritual healing paradigm'. Here crystals, especially clear quartz stones, are used to channel,

are used. The second method of crystal healing can be called the 'resonance placement paradigm'.

the resonance placement paradigm

This method doesn't require belief in the spirit worlds or in any kind of energy coming from elsewhere, but relies only on the power of the crystals themselves, and the healing intuition of an individual. Many different stones may be used, each one chosen for a particular beneficial effect on the patient. Placed on or around the body, the colour, shape and composition of the stones are thought to create a resonance that encourages healing to take place. This system parallels the magical, talismanic practices of carrying gemstones, as well as the Ayurvedic traditions of India in which stones are chosen to bring the most harmonious energy to each individual.

direct and amplify energy from the healer, or from the spiritual realms with which the healer works. Healing energy is mentally directed through the stone, which amplifies and clarifies the healing potential. Some North American Indian healers use quartz in this way to diagnose a problem and then remove it. In these instances the crystal may or may not come into contact with the patient. Very often only one or two crystals

△ **In all periods of history, crystals have been regarded as magical and otherworldly.**

▽ **As ideal examples of the universe's pattern-making and orderly structural harmony, crystals naturally bring clarity to the mind.**

▽ **The clarity of crystal can be felt to positively influence the space within which it is placed.**

Getting to know your crystals

Each human being is completely unique, and we will all respond to a specific crystal's energy in a different way. Getting to know each crystal in your own collection is very important. It is more helpful to learn how to get to know the feel of an individual stone than to learn what other collectors or crystal experts have to say about it. What the body senses or knows, our intuition can be trained to access. The most effective healer uses information from a combination of sources, but the most important source is the physical and mental personal experience of healer and patient.

learning a new stone

Once you have gathered together a small collection of crystals you need to begin to learn their potential. Cleanse all new stones well before working with them. Begin by holding a new stone in one hand for a

moment or two, then in the other. Notice how you are feeling. Remember that all the information you can get from the crystal's energy will be registered inside you. Get used to recognizing changes of feeling in your body, emotions and mind.

◁ Taking time to examine your crystals creates a strong intuitive energy link that will be useful in healing situations. It isn't necessary to always have new insights or experiences in this process.

△ Lay out your entire collection on a neutral coloured background. Gazing quietly at a selection of stones will help identify the effect that each stone creates.

After holding the stone for a moment, place it away from you and simply gaze at it. Pick it up once more and notice any changes within you. Close your eyes and simply sit with the stone, then, once more, place it away from you. By such processes you will gradually see a pattern emerging. Once you have established your own responses to a stone you will be able to begin by experience and experiment to find out whether your own response is shared by other people.

The next stage of getting to know your crystals is to place a stone at an energy sensitive spot such as a chakra. This can give you some further insight. Place the stone for a minute or two on each chakra in turn and take notes on your responses. You might find that some places, and some stones, are a lot more sensitive than others.

Keep a stone with you for a while to deepen your connection with it, especially if it is a new one. Putting one under your pillow or next to you when you sleep may produce significant dreams, particularly if you have a clear intention before you fall asleep that you wish to learn the properties of a stone. Again, make a note of these experiences. Carry a stone around with you for a few days and then leave it at home for a while. As you repeat this process you may notice changes in how you feel, or behave or in how others are behaving towards you.

▽ Holding a stone to a chakra point will show you how it may modify the energy of that centre.

MEDITATION WITH THE SENSES

Sit quietly with the stone you wish to explore just in front of you. Close your eyes and quieten your mind by focusing your attention on your breathing for a minute or two.

1 Pick up the crystal and hold it comfortably in your hands.

2 Imagine your awareness spiralling down into the stone, as it opens up and lets you explore it.

3 First see how, in your imagination, the inside of the stone feels. Is there a sense of texture, a change of temperature, a sense of space or restriction?

4 Is there any sense of sound? If the energy within the crystal were expressed as sound, how would it seem to you?

5 Breathe in the energy in your imagination. Does it remind you of anything? Is there a fragrance at all? Is there a quality of taste?

6 Visualize that you open the eyes of your imagination and that you can see the energy of the crystal around you. This may take any form, pattern, landscape, or figure.

7 When you have explored the stone enough simply close off your inner senses and bring your awareness back to your body and the sounds that are around you.

8 Complete the grounding process by seeing all aspects of your awareness spiralling back out of the stone and into your body.

9 Make a note of your experiences.

Building your collection

Until recently jewellery shops and specialist mineralogical shops were the only places where samples of crystal and uncut gemstones could be found. But with the growth of interest in crystals, both as a fashion accessory and as a way to encourage self-development, it has now become a lot easier to build up a good collection. Mind, body and spirit exhibitions, alternative healing shows and New Age shops usually have crystals for sale. There are also mail order companies that will supply stones. It is always a good idea to look around as much as possible before buying, to check out the range of quality and price.

selecting your stones

Start your collection with stones that attract you. Being drawn to a crystal by its appearance or by some intuitive prompting is the easiest way to identify stones that are

▽ A global market means that crystals from many different countries are available.

△ The craftsmen of the Far East, Brazil and Germany have had long experience in cutting and carving decorative crystal pieces.

▽ A characteristic crystal of smoky quartz with flat faces meeting at precise angles.

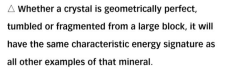

△ Whether a crystal is geometrically perfect, tumbled or fragmented from a large block, it will have the same characteristic energy signature as all other examples of that mineral.

△ Pearls are formed within the shells of sea or freshwater oysters from layers of calcium carbonate with organic compounds. They are among the most precious of gems.

◁ Red coral is another precious organic gemstone with a long history of healing use.

of use to you. Pay attention, too, to stones you really dislike. These will be important as they express qualities you do not wish to face. They may work at deep levels that would be inappropriate for you to focus on just now.

Crystals come in many different forms, and each has its uses. Mineralogical samples are crystals in their natural form, showing the way in which they have grown and the base rock (or 'matrix') upon which they rest. Single crystals have usually been separated from the matrix and surrounding material. Often a single crystal will have one natural, faceted termination (or 'point'), while the other end is rough or broken. These crystals will usually be of attractive appearance and relatively undamaged.

Fragments of large or damaged crystals are often sold as tumbled stones. Tumbling imitates the natural weathering of running water. The pieces are slowly polished as they turn in revolving drums with different

grades of abrasive gravel. The end product is a smooth, polished and highly coloured sample of crystal. Buying tumbled stones is often the cheapest way of building up a crystal collection, and tumbled stones have the added advantage of having no delicate edges and faces to get damaged. Larger pieces of crystal can be cut and polished into a variety of shapes, both decorative and practical. Each will retain the qualities of the mineral modified

by its new shape. For example, spheres can be useful for massage and give a gentle diffused field of energy. Pyramids or obelisks are much more directional and active in their energy fields.

Whatever selection you build up, it is a good idea to find out the basic physical properties of each stone. This will ensure you do not inadvertently damage pieces by mixing them with much harder crystals. Mineral identification guides will provide this information.

How to display your stones will depend on the way you use them. Small healing stones are best kept in a compartmentalized box or case. This allows you to group stones of a type or colour together. It is also easier to separate very soft crystals. Remember that even a small collection can weigh quite a lot so ensure that a working kit is in a sturdy box that you are able to carry around.

▽ It is important to find a safe, practical way of storing your crystals.

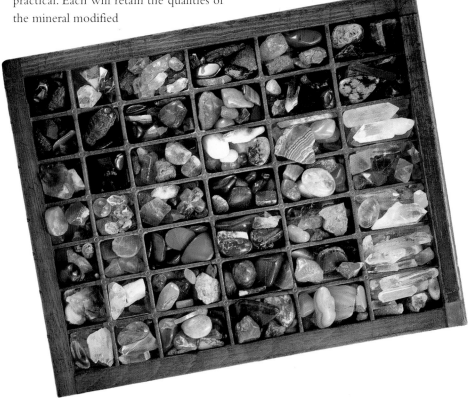

Cleansing crystals

Crystals need to be protected from physical damage, but also from energetic imbalances. Crystals can register a wide range of vibrations, from electricity and magnetism, to sound, emotions and thoughts. The natural coherence of crystal can eventually dissipate imbalances within the lattice but the following cleansing techniques speed this process and ensure only positive energy is present in healing situations.

Every cleansing method has advantages and disadvantages. You will quickly learn to determine the most useful method for your situation. It is better to regularly cleanse the crystals you are working with rather than letting imbalances accumulate over time.

cleansing with water and salt

With the exception of a few water-soluble minerals, each new crystal should be washed before you use it. Use a little soapy water to remove dust and fingerprints. Water will

▽ Use whichever cleansing techniques you find most effective and practical. You will soon learn to recognize the feel of a cleansed stone.

also cleanse your stones of energy imbalances. Another method is to hold the stones in cold running water and then leave them to dry naturally. Visualizing the flow of water drawing away all imbalances as you cleanse can speed up the process.

Salt water is often suggested as a medium for clearing crystal energies. Although effective, it can be difficult to remove all traces of salt from the tiny crevices in the crystal, and salt will damage the surface of many softer stones. Dry sea salt piled around each stone and left for a day is a good alternative. Either use small dishes for each stone or nestle each stone in its own little mound of salt on a large flat plate.

cleansing with sound

Resonant sound from a tuning fork, metal bowl or bell rapidly vibrates the physical structure of the crystal allowing it quickly to 'shake off' any intrusive energies. Simply hold a struck bell or tuning fork close to your stones, or place one or two crystals in the bottom of a Tibetan singing bowl, and run the wooden handle around the rim.

△ Use a clear intention that your chosen method will cleanse your stones, to speed the process.

▽ Mineralogy reference books will tell you which stones can be placed in water.

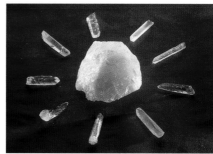

◁ Dry sea salt, without any extra additives, draws out negative energies. Throw the salt away after use.

△ Surrounding a crystal with other cleansed stones, or placing the stone on a large cluster or bed of crystal, is an effective cleansing method.

▽ Incense cones or sticks make sufficient smoke for cleansing as well as grains, resins and herbs.

enlivening crystals

To enliven a very tired crystal, it may be necessary to bury it in clay or the earth – but always be sure to mark the spot well! Leave in place for a day to a week before returning to check on progress.

energy cleansing

After cleaning, it is important to remove any energy imbalances your crystal may have accumulated. Over time crystals can be affected by strong negative emotions or electromagnetic pollution. Such a stone will feel lifeless, dull or unpleasant in some way no matter what its appearance. Energy cleansing can be done in many ways. The simplest method is to use incense smoke or a smudge stick with traditional cleansing herbs and pass the stone through the smoke until you feel it clear.

Sandalwood, frankincense, juniper and sage have a long history of use simply because they were found to be powerful purifying herbs. Experiment to find those that work best for your stones.

Get into the habit of cleansing your healing stones before and after use – and don't forget to cleanse any large decorative crystals you may have around your home from time to time.

Crystals and chakras

Gemstones were traditionally used to alleviate the physical symptoms of illness. Today, crystal healing focuses on removing the underlying energy imbalances that may eventually lead to physical problems. In modern complementary therapies, as well as many traditional forms of healing, the person is seen as a complex interaction of different sorts of energy systems. Though not so apparent as the physical body, these energy systems influence every aspect of our lives and they can be clearly felt by anyone trained to notice the subtle differences and states they produce.

△ Tiger's Eye is a variety of quartz that works well at the solar plexus chakra.

Ancient Indian seers perceived seven chakras – vortices of spinning energy along the spinal column, each with its own functions for maintaining health. They found exercises and meditations to regulate and enhance each chakra to promote spiritual wellbeing.

chakras and colours

The chakra system was simplified in the West and a single rainbow colour was attributed to each of the seven chakras. The colour correspondences of the chakra system can be combined with the colour of

△ Ruby, like all red stones, helps to energize and balance the first chakra at the base of the spine.

▽ Carnelian is coloured bright orange by iron particles. It helps balance the sacral chakra.

△ Moss agate is a green stone that works in harmony with the heart chakra.

▽ Turquoise is among the most-used light blue stones, which work with the throat chakra.

crystals for a simple healing system. Through observation, intuition or dowsing, a crystal therapist can determine which of the chakras need re-balancing to restore equilibrium to the system as a whole. Appropriate crystals can be placed around the energy centre, and, by the colour or some other balancing aspect of the crystal, that chakra will be brought back to a healthier functioning. This is an effective way of releasing physical, emotional and mental stress.

SIMPLE CHAKRA HEALING

Crystals that are the same colour as a chakra will enhance its natural qualities, whatever the situation. For a simple chakra balancing therapy, place one stone of the appropriate colour on each chakra area for a few minutes.

Use small tumbled stones or crystal points. Choose your stones and arrange them in sequence beside where you will be lying. When you are ready, you can easily pick up the stones and place them on your body without them falling off. If you prefer to sit, you will need small pieces of surgical tape to hold each stone in position on your body.

1 The first or base chakra is at the base of the spine. Use a black or red stone between your legs to balance physical energy, motivation and practicality, and to promote a sense of reality.

2 The second or sacral chakra is in the lower abdomen, below the navel. Use an orange stone here to balance creativity, and to release stress and blocks in your life that prevent enjoyment.

3 The third or solar plexus chakra is close to the bottom of the ribcage. Use a yellow or gold stone in this position to clear your thoughts, reduce anxiety and improve confidence.

4 The fourth or heart chakra is in the centre of the chest. Use a green stone here to balance your relationship with others and the world, to increase calm and create a sense of direction in life.

5 The fifth chakra is at the throat. Use a light blue stone here to ease communication difficulties, express yourself and bring peacefulness.

6 The sixth is the brow chakra in the centre of the forehead. Use a dark blue or indigo stone here, to increase understanding, access ideas and promote intuitive skills and memory.

7 The seventh chakra is the crown, situated just a little way above the top of the head. A violet stone placed in this position integrates and balances all aspects of the self – physical, mental, emotional and spiritual.

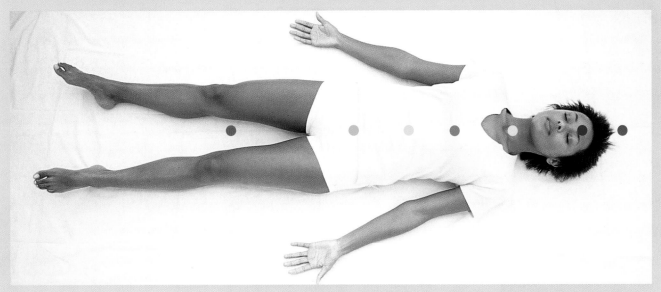

Subtle bodies

The subtle bodies are non-physical aspects of each human being surrounding and interpenetrating the body. They constitute what is usually called the aura. Each level of the aura can be thought of as the individual seen from a slightly different energy vibration – like listening to the different instruments playing in an orchestra.

different levels

Closest to the physical body in frequency is the etheric body, an exact double of the body and a template for the physical organs and systems. On a finer level is the emotional body, often perceived as a swirl of ever-changing colours that alters with our moods. The mental body contains thought processes, ideas and beliefs we hold about ourselves and the world. It usually appears as a yellow glow and can be bright around the head during concentration. The

▽ Dowsing can be used to choose the most appropriate crystal for healing. With the most useful stone or stones, the pendulum will rotate, while with others it will remain stationary.

finer vibrational subtle bodies contain the energy patterns of our spiritual natures and are less bound by rules of time and space.

Like the chakra system, the subtle bodies have a complex interaction and flow between them. When this is disrupted in some way it can create knock-on effects that may lead to the symptoms of stress and disease. Disruption in a subtle body can be likened to a storm that fails to dissipate and upsets the weather patterns for miles around – an El Niño in the body! The subtle bodies can also be imagined as many layers of glass letting light into a room. Dirt and dust accumulating on one layer will cast shadows on all the others and into the room itself. Crystals can be a very effective tool for removing these energy disruptions.

Subtle bodies are made up of fine energy frequencies so we need some way to detect them and then make accurate assessments of their condition. Using a crystal pendulum is the simplest method, amplifying the body's innate understanding of these subtle fields. Crystal pendulums will also help to restore most imbalances as they are located.

PENDULUM HEALING
Learning to use a crystal pendulum can be one of the easiest ways to work with the subtle bodies.

1 Suspend the crystal pendulum. In your mind, intend that the pendulum will begin to swing away from its resting position when there is an energy imbalance in the subtle bodies that it is able to correct.
2 Allow the pendulum to move whichever way it wants until it comes to rest once more. When this happens it indicates the balance has been completed.

▽ Any crystal can be used for dowsing but it is best to start with a stone that has a broad healing ability such as clear quartz or amethyst.

FIVE-LINE CLEARING

This is a technique that can be used to restore balance to all the subtle bodies. It is not necessary to know what imbalances are being cleared where the pendulum begins to move away from the neutral swing. All subtle bodies interpenetrate and affect each other. An area of imbalance may be at only one level or it may move through many different layers. Simply focus on the pendulum movement and move steadily up the body on each line.

This technique is an excellent way to help others. A clear quartz or amethyst will give the best results because they act on very broad levels, and work as all-purpose healers. Stones such as garnet or lapis lazuli will focus their balancing abilities in more precise ways.

To help you to make the correct movements with the pendulum, imagine five lines running down your partner's body: one in the centre – the midline – and two either side, running parallel. The inner two lines should be within the outline of the body, the outer two lines are just outside the physical body.

1 Put the crystal pendulum into a neutral backwards and forwards swing. With the patient lying down, suspend the pendulum a few centimetres above the body at the midline, in the centre of the body, just below the feet.

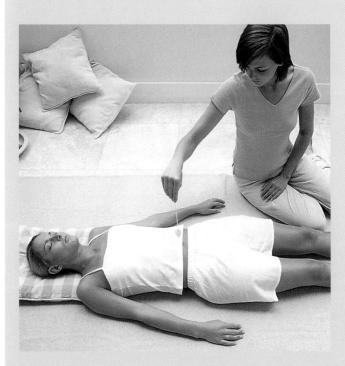

2 Slowly move the swinging pendulum up the midline. Wherever there is a movement away from the neutral swing, stay there until the pendulum returns to normal. Move up the midline until you reach the top of the head.

3 Start the process again, this time moving the pendulum up one side of the body, and then the other. Finally, move the pendulum up the fourth and fifth lines, just to the outside of the physical body.

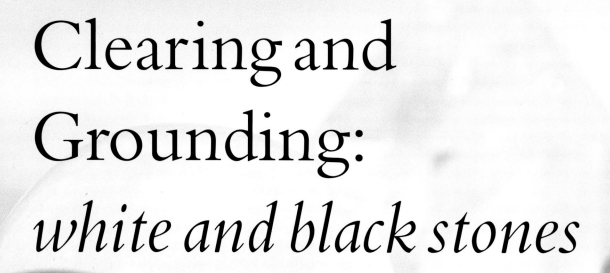

Clearing and Grounding:
white and black stones

Stones that are clear or white in colour have the
ability to bring clarity and purity to the aura.
This makes them very useful healing tools.
Black and other dark coloured stones help to
integrate the healing that has taken place so that
we can feel the practical effects of the process.
They help to strengthen and stabilize our
fundamental energies.

Clear quartz – solidified light

Quartz (SiO_2) is the commonest and most widespread mineral in the earth's crust. It is a component of many types of rock and a constituent of many different minerals. The purest variety of quartz is known as rock crystal and has the clarity, transparency and coolness of ice.

Quartz can form as magnificent clusters of crystal, as gigantic single crystals and as massive aggregates. Impurities and inclusions of other minerals give the quartz family the greatest variety of any crystal. Quartz is very weather-resistant and with the erosion of bedrock it finds its way down rivers where it becomes the main component of river and seashore pebbles – as well as of sands and gravels.

△ Clear quartz is completely transparent and colourless except for internal fractures and microscopic bubbles of gas or water that appear as milky areas.

▽ Quartz can form in a huge variety of beautiful clusters, aggregates and single stones.

DIRECTING ENERGY

A single quartz crystal anywhere within the aura will help to bring balance. It often helps to visualize the flow of energy you want and place the quartz appropriately. A quartz point above the head and another between the feet creates a useful flow up or down the body. Points facing downwards have a grounding effect. Points turned upwards give a feeling and quality of expansion. Another method is to hold pointed quartz in your hands. The left hand (in right-handed people) is receptive and absorbing, the right is projecting and energizing. It's the other way round for left-handed people.

1 Hold a quartz point inwards with your absorbing hand and another with its point outwards in your energizing hand to create a flow through the body that balances and clears energy blocks.
2 Change the direction of the crystals after a few minutes and see how you feel.

◁ Transparent, clear crystals have always held immense fascination. To hold solid matter and yet be able to see through it is a truly magical experience.

types of clear quartz

Clear quartz normally grows long six-sided crystals, meeting at a natural point or termination. Opposite the termination, the base of the crystal grows from 'massive quartz', which consists of microscopic crystals, or a bedrock of some other mineral. Quartz with its point towards the body has a tendency to energize, whereas quartz with points away from the body releases or discharges excess or unwanted energy. Large flat crystals called tabular quartz also act as rapid transporters and transmuters of energy. Rough pieces, tumbled and smooth-polished quartz give a less directional, more diffuse effect that can be useful for gently infusing energy at one place.

Some quartz crystal shapes can focus or amplify energy many times above the usual. Laser wands are so called because they have slightly bent sides that narrow significantly towards a small termination. Energy

△ Herkimer diamonds, placed under a pillow at night, can help to encourage lucid dreaming.

entering the base becomes compressed and more energetic as it moves up the crystal towards the tip. These crystals can be powerful healing tools.

Herkimer diamonds

The most brilliant quartz crystals are called Herkimer diamonds. First found in Herkimer County, New York State, USA they are particularly clear and bright. They are powerful cleansers renowned for their ability to enhance subtle perceptions. Herkimer diamonds encourage stabilization and a dynamic exchange of energy.

Clear quartz, of any shape, is very useful in crystal work because it amplifies and increases the harmony of all energies with which it is brought into contact. The coherence of rock crystal strengthens all the energy systems of the body, bringing stability and calmness to the mind. It can also direct energy from one site to another.

THE SEAL OF SOLOMON

One of the simplest and most widely applicable layouts using clear quartz is called the Seal of Solomon. Some stones may need to be taped in place, some may be on and some off the body. This layout can also be used for localized healing – simply repeat the process with crystals placed around the area that you feel needs help.

1 Choose six natural crystals of equal size and arrange them, evenly spaced, in a hexagon shape around the body. Start off with the points facing outwards, this will help to release stresses and imbalances.
2 After a few minutes, turn the crystals round so the points face inwards. This re-energizes the body at every level.

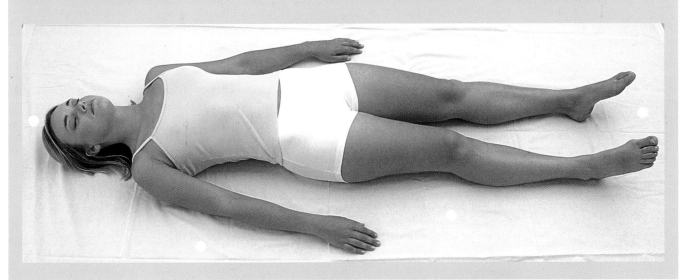

Moonstone and selenite – moonlight and water

Moonstone and selenite each have a soft, luminescent quality and are associated with both moonlight and water because of the way the light plays on their surface.

moonstone

A variety of the common mineral feldspar, moonstone ($KaSi_3O_8$) has a soft, lustrous translucence of white, yellow or pink. Moonstone can sometimes have a rich play of colour, in which case it is called rainbow moonstone. In India, moonstone has long been regarded as the perfect gemstone for women. It is well known for easing menstrual cramps and other constrictions

△ Moonstone is recognized by its translucent sheen, no matter what colour it may be.

▽ Selenite is a very soft stone made up of thin layers of gypsum that diffuse the light.

within the female reproductive system – carry a moonstone in your hip pocket to help relieve the symptoms of PMT. It is understood that emotional stress upsets the body's natural fluid balance. Moonstone helps to balance all fluid systems in the body, such as the lymphatic and digestive systems.

Emotional states are linked to the element of water, which is ruled by the moon. This is why the moon's gemstone is able to work so effectively in these areas.

△ Holding a piece of selenite helps to drain any negativity from the body.

Moonstone will gently stabilize all emotional states and help to release any stress and tension. These qualities link moonstone to the sacral chakra, which is a focus for emotional tension. Moonstone also works well at the solar plexus, where emotional stress can disrupt the nervous system and the digestion of food.

MOON NET

To experience the soothing effects of moonstone, choose five pieces of about the same size.

1 Place one moonstone on the front of each hipbone. You may need to tape the stones in place. Place another moonstone on the front in the dip of each shoulder.

2 Place one just touching the top of the head.

3 After a little while there will be a deep relaxation and a soothing energy washing through the body. After five to ten minutes, remove the stones and remain easy for a little while. Creativity and intuition may also be enhanced.

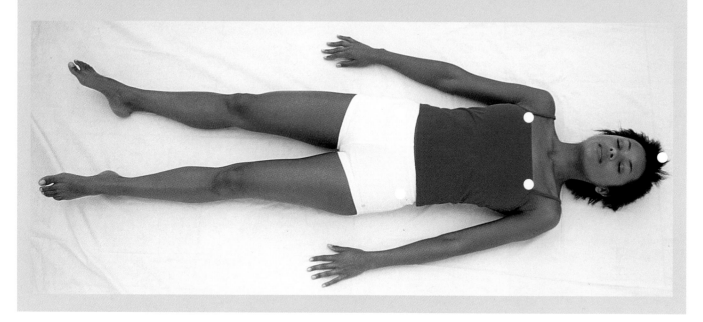

selenite

A clear transparent form of gypsum, selenite ($CaSO_4.2H_2O$) is a very soft mineral easily scratched by a fingernail. Gypsum is so water-sensitive that even a change of humidity can make it bend. The thin layers or stripes visible in selenite create its moon-like luminescence. Such a delicate mineral needs careful care and handling, but it is well worth the effort. Few other crystals have the ability to effortlessly remove unwanted energies from the subtle bodies. Selenite combines the soothing effects of moonstone with the energy shifting properties of crystals with parallel striations (stripes). Whenever there are build-ups of energy, such as inflammation and pain, selenite brings a cooling release.

clearing negativity

Selenite is a very common mineral that crystallizes in long blade-like shapes. Although it can be tumbled and shaped into wands or spheres, it is really so delicate that the finest quality stones should be collector's pieces rather than used in everyday healing.

When a stressful experience seems to be locked into the mind or the emotions, causing continual repetition of the same thoughts or feelings, selenite can be used to break that negative cycle.

Sit quietly for a moment and observe where the energy of the experience seems to be located. Somewhere in the body there will be an unusual sense of heaviness or dullness, or possibly an ache of some kind. Take a few minutes to see how sensations and thoughts revolve around the area. The selenite can now be used to drain the negative energy away. Either place the crystal on that spot and visualize the stone drawing away the source of stress, or hold the selenite in your hands and visualize the negative energy flowing and concentrating into the crystal and then rapidly streaming outwards to a place where it can be of use.

All soft minerals absorb imbalances rapidly and will need good cleaning after use. Do not use water with selenite. Sound or incense smoke cleansing will be effective.

▽ **Moonstone works where there is emotional or physical tension or blocks in energy flow.**

More white and clear stones

Transparent or clear stones exhibit the qualities of amplifying and clarifying. White stones can show the same characteristics, but they tend to be gentler in their actions. Milky quartz, for example, has the same structure as rock crystal, but the presence of many microscopic air bubbles reflects all light back from the interior. Milky quartz has a gentle energizing and soothing effect that radiates out into its surroundings.

Some agates, particularly Botswana agate, have a high proportion of white or light blue-grey banding. These are created by different sized quartz crystals, impurities and

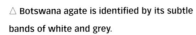
△ Botswana agate is identified by its subtle bands of white and grey.

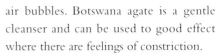
◁ Milky quartz may seem less attractive than the clear variety but it is equally helpful as a healing tool.

▽ Agate slices show the formation of the crystal as different bands of coloured quartz.

air bubbles. Botswana agate is a gentle cleanser and can be used to good effect where there are feelings of constriction.

diamond

The strength and brilliance of diamond (C_4) has made it the world's most valuable gemstone. Diamonds are octahedral crystals of pure carbon found in many colours as well as clear. Most single diamonds are found in soil deposits along river banks. Large deposits of diamonds, found in hard igneous rock, are rare and difficult to work.

Diamonds were first mined in quantity in South Africa in the 19th century, and South African mines have produced more diamonds than any others throughout history. Most coloured diamonds are used in industry: less than a quarter of all finds are of the completely transparent quality that is required by the gem trade. This means that coloured diamond crystals are reasonably priced, though they are still quite difficult to obtain.

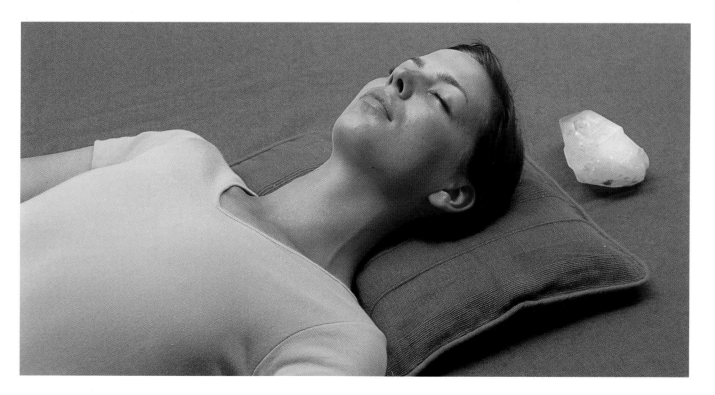

△ Clear stones have a natural affinity with the crown chakra. Both are able to reflect the whole spectrum of energy.

Diamond is primarily an amplifier of energy and is best used to enhance the properties of other stones. It is also a very effective detoxifying stone, effective at removing stagnant and inappropriate energies from the body. Diamond has a natural affinity with the crown chakra and has been found to help realign the bones of the head, the jaw and spine. It can be used to adjust small imbalances in the bones of the skull that may have been created after dental work, for example.

other transparent stones

Most crystals have a natural transparent form though this may be quite rare, as the impurities that enter a crystal lattice only need to be present in minute amounts to create colour. The clear form of any mineral can be used at the crown chakra above the top of the head. Simply placing the stone here will stimulate all the energy bodies and help remove imbalances.

Danburite ($CaB_2Si_2O_8$) is a brilliant clear stone that forms wedge-shaped crystals with parallel striations like those in topaz. It is light and fairly fragile, but is a useful activating and cleansing stone that amplifies and brightens the energies of other stones.

Apophyllite ($KCa_4\ Si_8O_{20}(F,OH).\ 8H_2O$) has greater brilliance than danburite but is even softer and lighter. The crystals tend to be cube-based or pyramidal with bright shiny surfaces. Apophyllite allows us to become more aware of subtle perceptions and can be an effective meditation crystal, expanding awareness while helping release blocks and stresses. The green variety encourages awareness of levels within nature.

Softer still is calcite ($CaCO_3$), a very common mineral that can sometimes be found as perfectly transparent crystals known as Iceland spar. All calcite is a good remover of stagnant energy and this too can be a useful meditation tool.

▽ Danburite is light and brilliant, amplifying the energy of stones around it.

▽ Apophyllite is mined in Poona, western India. It can be brilliantly clear or translucent green.

▽ Calcite, when perfectly clear, is called Iceland Spar. It commonly forms rhomboidal prisms.

Smoky quartz – the solidifier

Smoky quartz (SiO_2) ranges from a light golden brown to deep black. Even when it is very dark, smoky quartz nearly always remains translucent. The colour is thought to be derived from natural sources of radioactivity close to where the crystals are formed. Smoky quartz carries the same basic energy as clear quartz but absorbs and stores it rather than radiating it. This gives the crystal a quietening and calming quality that makes it a help in focusing energy internally. The absorbing quality of smoky quartz makes it an excellent stone for meditation as it stabilizes the body and mind.

▷ **Smoky quartz is much less common than the clear, milky, or gem-quality varieties.**

TO BRING CALM

Smoky quartz, with its quiet, calming energy is an effective grounding stone. As it draws energy towards itself it can remove imbalances from the subtle energy bodies, gently dissolving and transmuting negativity. This simple stone placement will help to collect all sorts of scattered and confused energies. It helps bring emotional calm and clarity of mind and allows any overabundance of energy to flow out into the earth.

1 Use two smoky quartz crystals. If possible use crystals that have natural points (terminations). This helps to move the energy in the most appropriate direction. Place one with its point down the body at the base of the throat where the collarbones meet the breastbone.

2 Place the other with its point downwards between the legs, either between the knees or between the feet. Stay like this for five minutes or until you feel fully grounded.

GROUNDING STONES

The placement of a grounding stone during and after a crystal healing session, or holding one in your hand, really helps to integrate the changes into the physical body. Without proper grounding any benefits may disappear as soon as normal activity resumes. Grounding stones can be placed at any of the following locations:

1 At groin points on the front of the hips
2 At or near the base of the spine
3 Between the legs
4 By the insides of the knees
5 Between the feet
6 Below each foot

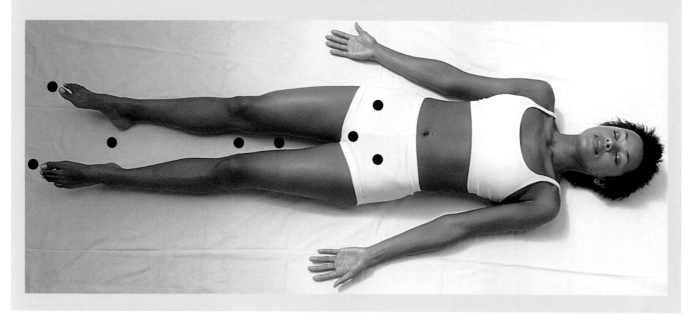

achieving stability

Balance in life is essential. Outward, dynamic change needs to be countered by stability, focus and centredness. As most healing work is concerned with the removal of inappropriate energy it tends to initiate deep levels of energy adjustment throughout many subtle systems of the body. Any rearrangement of energy, no matter how beneficial eventually, can create turbulence in everyday life, bringing confusion, emotional instability and lack of focus. To avoid this discomfort, healers take care to emphasize grounding and centring techniques to act as an anchor, stabilizing and balancing the changes that healing creates. Grounding ensures a firm contact with the energies of the planet so that excess energy can be conducted away from the body. It focuses on the present moment, practicality and connectedness to reality.

Being centred suggests that the focus of awareness is balanced within the whole body – rather than just being in the head. There is awareness of the world outside, yet there is no confusion or distraction. It is not possible to be grounded effectively without being centred, and it is not possible to be centred unless our energies are grounded.

The first chakra at the base of the spine is concerned with centring and grounding. Techniques that direct energy and attention to this point and to points on the legs and feet are naturally grounding. Red, brown and black stones all help in directing and stabilizing energy in the body.

◁ **Confusion and anxiety can be rapidly reduced by holding a grounding stone.**

▷ **Red stones can also help to achieve stability, and can be used with black stones for grounding.**

Black tourmaline – alignment

Extremely useful for protecting and grounding personal energy, tourmaline $(\mathrm{Na(Mg,Fe,Li,Mn,Al)_3Al_6(BO_3)_3Si_6O_{18}(OH,F)_4})$ can be found in nearly every colour and the same crystal will often contain several different colours. Black tourmaline is known as schorl. It is easy to recognize with its long, thin striated sides with three

▷ Tourmaline commonly crystallizes alongside quartz and often interpenetrates it. Tourmaline quartz (or tourmalated quartz) combines the qualities of both stones, clearing and grounding, energizing and protecting.

EARTH NET

A strong energy connection to the earth is a prerequisite for effective grounding and protective support. An energy net using eight black tourmalines can be used to reinforce this support, and can be particularly useful after moving house or travelling. Indeed, there have been reports that black tourmaline can reduce the effects of jetlag. One of the effects of tourmaline particularly emphasized in this layout is the ability to help the bones realign themselves. Tensions in bone and muscle are relaxed and physical balance improves. Tinnitus, the continuous ringing of the ears, has many causes, but misaligned skull bones can add to the problem. Wearing tourmaline earrings has been found to help this.

1 Use a green cloth as a background to lie on, or a white sheet for second choice. If possible arrange it so that your head will be to the north.

2 Put four tourmalines pointing inwards in a cross – one above the head, one between the feet and the others at either side, midway down the body.

3 Place the remaining four tourmalines just to the right of the others at an angle of about 20 degrees, so all are aligned to the same imaginary point in the centre of the body.

4 Remain in the energy net for five to ten minutes, then when you have removed the crystals spend at least 15 minutes resting before returning to normal activity.

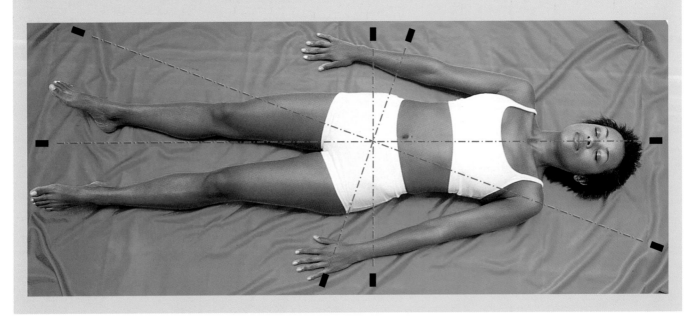

◁ Far left: tourmaline earrings can help in a wide range of situations, protecting the energy of the wearer. Tourmaline is thought to be able to help ease the symptoms of tinnitus.

◁ After using crystals for a healing session they should always be cleaned. Place tourmalines in a bowl of fresh water and leave for 2-3 hours.

faces giving it a triangular cross-section. When tourmaline is heated, it produces a positive electrical charge at one end and a negative charge at the other, making it a useful switching device in a lot of heat sensitive equipment.

energy focus

As a grounding stone, black tourmaline can be used whenever energies are scattered and confused. It will very quickly bring the awareness back to the present moment. Because of this, the stone gives strong protection against negativity of all sorts. A negative influence is anything that superimposes itself and overrides the individual's own energy field to create imbalance. A crystal that reinforces personal energy will help against these disruptive effects. Black tourmaline deflects negativity back into the earth, rather than absorbing the energy into itself, where it would accumulate and interfere with its efficiency.

TOURMALINE CIRCUIT

Crystals that have parallel striations running along their lengths tend to be very good at moving energy from one place to another, releasing blocks and tensions in the body. Sometimes the same problem resurfaces many times because a hidden, underlying block prevents effective healing. A pattern of black tourmaline crystals can clear away these deep levels of imbalance. Some stones in the pattern will be on the torso and hips, others will be put next to the head, shoulders, legs and feet. The number of crystals available to you will limit how and where they can be placed. Use dark tourmaline crystals – either black or very dark green. Alternatively, use smoky quartz.

1 Place the stones, all pointing in the same direction, in a figure of eight over and around your partner's body.
2 Emphasize the flow by tracing over the pattern with your hand, while holding another crystal.
3 After a few minutes within the pattern, remove the stones. Use another grounding stone to settle the energies before ending the session.

Obsidian – delving deep

Obsidian is volcanic glass that solidifies so rapidly from lava that it does not have time to form crystals. Although non-crystalline, obsidian often contains very small crystals of other minerals, particularly quartz, feldspar and iron compounds. These microcrystals can create variations of colour and lustre as light is reflected off them. The random scattering of light rays makes most obsidian black in appearance. Clusters of feldspar crystals create white or grey patches in snowflake obsidian. Iron minerals give the red-brown colour to mahogany obsidian, while densely packed crystals create a rainbow lustre or iridescence.

Obsidian is an effective grounding stone, but its most useful attribute is the ability to draw hidden imbalances to the surface and

▷ **Obsidian is black volcanic glass – ideal for transforming energy patterns.**

OBSIDIAN NET

This particular obsidian layout will allow the energies needed for cleansing and transformation to be gently integrated into the subtle bodies. Repeating this procedure regularly will bring about significant changes. You will need five obsidians and a red or black cloth to lie on.

1 Place one obsidian above the top of the head; two level with the neck/shoulder area; and two at the feet.
2 Lie within the net for three or four minutes. Then take as much time as you need before resuming normal activity, and sip a little water to help integration.

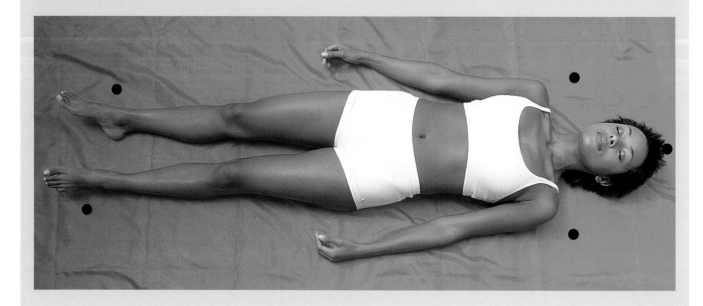

HOW TO SCRY

You will need an obsidian sphere (the size of the crystal does not matter), a black or dark-coloured cloth and a candle. The surface and structure of obsidian quietens normal thought processes, enabling the scryer temporarily to leave behind the rules of time and space. Set your crystal sphere or obsidian at a comfortable viewing distance from you. Surrounding the back of the stone with a dark cloth will help to prevent visual distractions. Make sure there are no reflections to distract you – dim light is best – such as the light of a single candle. Scrying involves all the senses, so don't expect to see visual imagery in the ball.

1 Gaze steadily at the sphere, without strain, looking through the crystal as if it were a window.

2 Frame a clear intention of what it is you wish to discover, then relax. You will feel the answer as a thought rather than an image.

△ Sipping a little water after any crystal healing will help to integrate the effects and ground and centre your energies.

release them. This needs to be done with some care as most hidden things are buried because they are uncomfortable to face. There are times when outdated patterns need to be broken to release the energy that is being wasted in supporting them. Obsidian is ideal when a transformation is needed, bringing fiery energy from deep within the earth to purify and cleanse.

scrying

Obsidian was one of the traditional materials used for scrying – seeing into the future. Scrying, or crystal gazing, is a worldwide practice that is used to reveal all sorts of information unknown to the conscious mind of the scryer. It has been known to reveal the causes and cures of illness, to explore and communicate with the spirit worlds and to foretell future events or disclose the truth of the past.

More black stones

Black stones have a solidifying and grounding effect on the human energy system. They increase our awareness of immediate reality and physicality.

haematite

This stone is a very common oxide of iron (Fe_2O_3). Large crystalline masses of haematite have an attractive silver sheen and are often cut for use in jewellery, though the stone is very brittle. Haematite is the main source of iron for industry, but there is also a soft variety formed in sedimentary rocks known as red ochre. This is the most ancient of precious materials, regarded the world over as a symbol of life-energy – the blood of the earth – and it is much sought after as a pigment.

Haematite is an energizer of the physical body but its primary use is as a grounding stone. Wearing or holding a piece of haematite will bring most people's awareness back to the body and the present almost instantly. Some individuals, however, find

▽ Haematite is one of the most effective grounding stones available.

RESTORING NATURAL BALANCE
We live in a very intense, artificially created electromagnetic environment. Treatment with a pendulum of lodestone or magnetite ensures that we do not suffer from the ill effects of strong electric fields. It is particularly useful for people who are over-sensitive to chemicals, who work with computers or other sources of electrical equipment or who are easily fatigued. Place a magnetite crystal or lodestone pendulum within a silver spiral on a length of cord or chain. Hold the stone a few centimetres above the body, and the pendulum will begin to rotate wherever there is an electromagnetic stress in the energy field. Hold the pendulum still until the rotation stops. The imbalance has now been removed.

Carrying a grounding stone will also help to prevent the unwanted accumulation of electromagnetic resonance. Holding the hands under cold running water, having a shower, wearing natural cloth and standing on the earth with bare feet are other ways of restoring natural balance.

▽ A lodestone pendulum will rotate when it approaches electromagnetic imbalances.

▽ A build-up of electromagnetic stress can be dissipated by running water.

that haematite has too energizing an effect and will need some less potent stone to ground them effectively.

magnetite and lodestone

Another iron ore, magnetite (Fe_3O_4) has the highest proportion of iron to be found in any mineral, making it very important commercially. Magnetite forms metallic grey octahedral crystals. Lodestone is the name given to the magnetic iron ore in its massive (microcrystalline) form. Lodestone and magnetite are extremely useful healing tools. They can align the chakras and subtle bodies allowing rapid release of stress and tension.

Because of their composition (iron and oxygen) and because they have a strong magnetic field, magnetite and lodestone both help to align us with the earth's own electromagnetic fields. This has a very

△ Jet is found washed up on shorelines after it has been dislodged from ancient seabeds.

▽ An octahedral crystal of magnetite (far left) with a piece of lodestone within a spring spiral ready for pendulum use.

grounding effect and brings an increased sense of belonging and security. The many energies along the spine can be strengthened by placing a small lodestone near the base chakra and another at the base of the skull. When you are healing someone, move a single stone slowly along their back a few centimetres above the spine. Take time to hold the stone still over areas that feel particularly sensitive or are uncomfortable.

jet

Like coal, jet is fossilized wood. Jet is formed when ancient waterlogged wood is compacted by vast pressure below the sea. It is found in several parts of the world. Like amber, jet produces static electricity when rubbed. This lightweight dark brown or black shiny gemstone exhibits grounding properties associated with its colour and the supportive, balancing qualities of the original source, trees. Valued for its protecting and comforting qualities in the 19th century, it was worn during mourning.

USING JET TO ENERGIZE THE CHAKRAS

Jet placed by the lower spine energizes the base chakra. When placed higher up the body it can draw energy from the base into those areas. Jet is valuable in chakra balancing, particularly if the upper chakras are under-energized when compared to the lower centres. Indications of this sort of imbalance are: plenty of energy and drive, but inability to use it creatively; confusion; frustration.

1 Place grounding stones under the feet and between the legs. At the groin points, use two black or red stones to stabilize the base chakra.
2 Place jet on under-energized areas and check after a few minutes if the balance is better.
3 Repeating this regularly for five minutes at a time will help to alleviate imbalance.

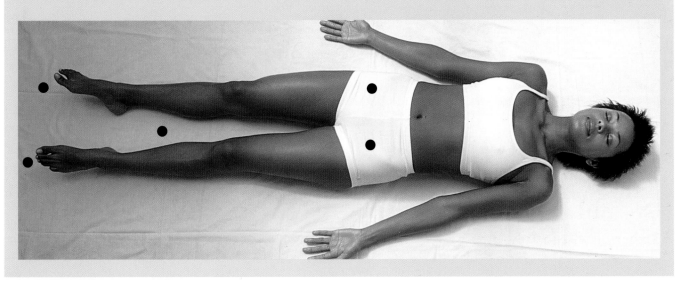

Energizing and Organizing: *red, orange and yellow stones*

Crystals from the warm end of the colour spectrum help to balance the first three chakras and release pent-up energy in the heart chakra. Stability, creativity and clear thinking, as well as the flow of life-energy through the physical body, are maintained by their properties.

Garnet – stone of fire

A large and chemically diverse group of silicate minerals, garnets come in a variety of colours, a rich wine-red being the most familiar. All stones of this colour used to be known as carbuncles, from the Latin *carbunculus* meaning small, red-hot coal.

Garnets form at very high temperatures in many different rocks, often in those altered by close proximity to volcanic activity. As it is a hard mineral, garnet survives erosion and is found in riverbeds and gravels. Its hardness and durability makes garnet ideal for abrasives and polishing.

There are many green, orange and brown garnets but the red varieties are the most useful in crystal healing work. Garnet is the finest energizing stone for the body. Especially when cut, it can amplify and energize the properties of other stones. Cut faceted stones of most crystals increase the liveliness of the stone and can act like a lens, focusing light with more intensity.

The fiery garnet can be placed wherever a lack of energy exists. It can act as a 'starter motor' for the body's repair mechanisms, so

▽ Tumbled garnets can be so dark as almost to show no colour, but the dense weight gives a clue to their identity.

very often garnet needs to be in place for just a short while to do its work. Where there is an area of underactive or stagnant energy, place a garnet at the centre of the body and surround it with four clear quartz crystals, points facing outwards, to help increase energy and distribute it.

△ The name garnet derives from the Greek word for pomegranate. The small, bright red crystals resemble the seeds of that fruit.

▽ A garnet surrounded by clear quartz points, with points facing outwards, will rebalance a 'cool' spot in the aura.

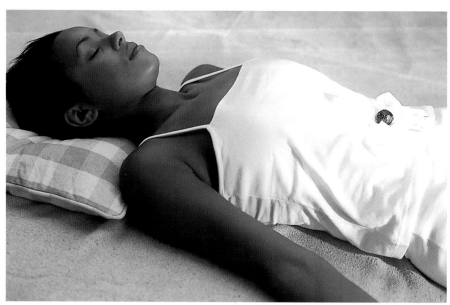

BODY SCANNING

Identifying areas of poor energy flow is a useful skill to learn. It relies upon the healer's sensitivity to slight changes in the patient's aura. Everyone will have different ways of registering energy changes, so just be attentive. Low energy can often feel like a dip, hollow or emptiness in the aura. It may feel cool or somehow 'wrong'. You may sense the difference in your hand or arm or be struck by an intuitive thought or emotional impression. If you are not sure of your assessment, just repeat the body scan a few more times. Even without consciously registering it, the body scan will give you enough information at deeper levels of the mind to place healing stones appropriately. Learn to trust your intuition. Using grounding stones will help reduce any doubt.

1 First sensitize your hands by rubbing them together or rolling a clear quartz crystal between your palms. Now bring your palms together slowly from a distance, and you should feel a tingling or a pressure as your hands come closer together. Gently 'bouncing' the space between your palms helps to

▽ **To increase your sensitivity in a scan, hold a clear quartz crystal in your scanning hand.**

build up your energy aura and your sensitivity to other energy fields.

2 Starting from near the feet and moving upwards, use one hand to slowly sweep a few centimetres above the patient's body. Your intention is to locate areas of blocked energy or under-energy. Simply move your hand through the aura and be open to any changes you may feel.

3 Where you have identified low energy, place a red, orange or yellow

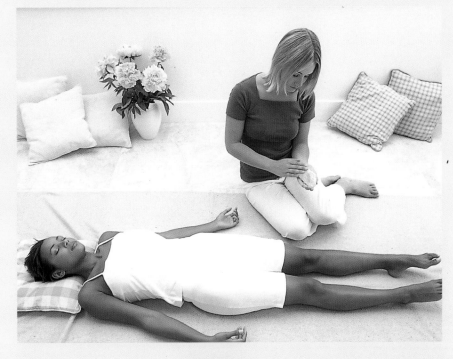

stone, whichever feels most appropriate, for a few minutes. Then, remove the stones and repeat the body scan. There should now be an improvement in the energy field. If a few areas of imbalance remain make a note of them and then repeat the process after a few days.

▽ **Before beginning any kind of scan, sensitize your own hands, and centre and ground your energies.**

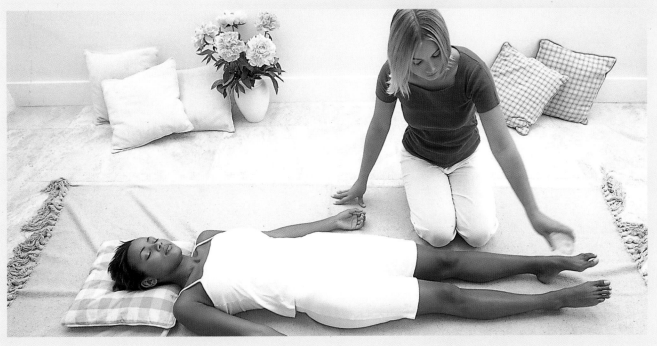

Ruby – motivation and action

Ruby is the red variety of the very hard mineral corundum (aluminium oxide, Al_2O_3), which takes its colour from traces of chromium and forms characteristic barrel-shaped crystals. Ruby has a long history of use as a gemstone, though until recently, because of its hardness, the stone was not faceted but was always polished into a domed, cabochon shape. In Ayurvedic Indian healing traditions ruby is the stone of the sun.

the heart

As the sun is the centre of the solar system so the heart is the centre of the physical body. Ruby balances the heart, enhancing its function and the circulation of the blood and improving the quality of thought and feeling associated with the heart – confidence, security, self-esteem and our relationship with others. Ruby acts by energizing us at the very centre of our being. It balances by reminding us of the

△ **Ruby has a hexagonal cross-section and usually forms barrel-shaped crystals.**

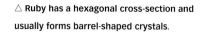

◁ **Polished ruby shows metal-like striations across its surface. Only the finest gem-quality rubies are translucent and deep red.**

vast reservoirs of energy within us that can enable us to succeed in any venture where we have full trust in our own abilities.

Red is the energy of gravity, pulling things together and establishing reality. Red is also the colour relating to the creation of matter and its manifestation. So it makes sense that a red stone such as ruby can help us to achieve our goals, particularly as ruby has such a connection with the heart, the seat of our desires.

RELEASING THE HEART'S POTENTIAL

This net will help release pent-up energy in the heart, remove guilt and unworthiness, and reveal your true strengths and potential. If possible have a white sheet to lie on, this encourages a gentle cleansing of negative emotions. Place a small ruby crystal at the heart chakra in the middle of the chest. Place 12 clear quartz crystals, points outwards, equally spaced around the body. Lie in the net for about five minutes.

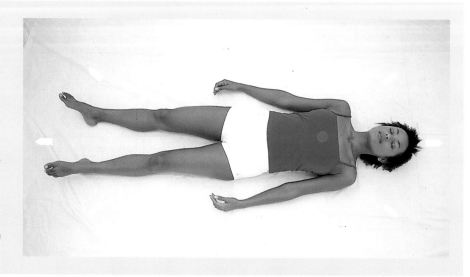

▷ **A ruby that has been polished into a traditional cabochon shape.**

Often in life the heart suffers pain because we feel unable to fulfil our wishes or desires. After pain such as this we often create barriers in an attempt to prevent future hurt. Unfortunately, what this really does is just separates us further from the source of our own power and courage.

Crystal healing techniques are ideal to help us solve such long-standing difficulties and barriers in our lives. Regular practice for five or ten minutes once or twice a week will begin to bring about positive change without having to revisit, and perhaps open, old wounds. In a situation where there is a loss of personal power, taking the initiative to help yourself is very important.

SUN NET

When there is a fear of failure, the heart, whose natural energy needs to expand outwards and experience life, becomes restricted. Then there is a lack of security, which comes from having lost the sense of being centred in the self. This happens at a mental and emotional level, but can also manifest in physical symptoms such as poor circulation, cold hands and feet and other upsets to the temperature regulation of the body. Ruby can be an ideal healing stone in these circumstances. To amplify and integrate the energy of the sun net lie on a yellow cloth.

This net will be gently energizing, bringing focus and clarity to the mind and emotions. It can be useful to help regulate the circulatory system and usually produces a gentle warming sensation. Use six small ruby crystals – stones that are not of gem quality are inexpensive and fine to use.

1 Place one ruby crystal above the head and one below the feet in the middle.

2 Place one ruby crystal next to each arm and one next to each knee so that the six stones are all evenly spaced around the body. Stay in this position for five to ten minutes.

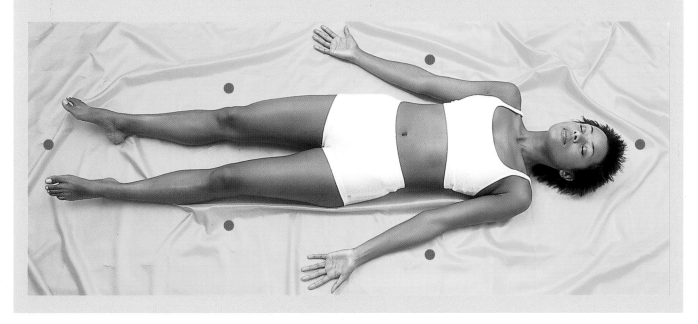

More red stones

Every red stone will give an energizing, activating and warming quality. Differences of crystal shape, quality of colour and chemical composition will affect the way each stone is experienced.

red jasper

This stone is actually a form of quartz (SiO_2) that crystallizes from hot solutions and is changed several times by reheating. This process produces a wide range of internal colour and patterning that makes jasper a valuable gemstone. Unlike other microcrystalline quartzes, jasper has a strong permanent colour created by iron minerals.

As an opaque, massive variety of quartz, red jasper focuses on solidity and grounding. It is an ideal stone to balance the base chakra. Jasper will always emphasize practical, down-to-earth solutions, which, like each piece of the stone, are unique to the individual. Jasper can also be coloured by impurities that turn it yellow and green.

△ Each piece of jasper is unique in its patterning and colour. Fractures in older crystals are refilled with quartz of a slightly different colour.

▽ Red coral helps to balance the base chakra, regulating physical strength, and the skeletal and circulatory systems.

red coral

The earth's surviving natural growths of red coral ($CaCO_3$) are now largely protected from exploitation but this strikingly coloured organic secretion, the home of colonies of tiny sea creatures, has long been regarded as a precious gemstone. In Ayurvedic tradition red coral is the best stone for the energies of the planet Mars. In Asia and America turquoise and red coral have been put together in wonderful designs for ceremonial and decorative jewellery. Old red coral beads can still be found, though imitations are very common.

Coral primarily acts as a balance for the emotions – its watery origins suggest this function – and it will work well for the maintenance of energy levels, enthusiasm and practicality.

fire opal

Opal ($SiO_2.nH_2O$) forms when hot silica-rich solutions fill the crevices of sedimentary rock. It is quartz with a high water content. All opals work well to balance the emotions. Fire opal is a deep orange-red, due to iron and manganese, which suggests a warming, activating quality. It is useful in emotional situations where there has been exhaustion, withdrawal and 'switching off'.

spinel

Iron and chromium impurities often give spinel ($MgAl_2O_4$) a deep ruby red coloration. Many of the famous larger 'rubies' of the world are, in fact, spinels. Spinels commonly form spiky octahedral crystals, which give them their name – 'little thorns' in Italian. The brown or orange-red varieties encourage the energizing properties of the base chakra. Spinel may also help with detoxification as its red energy will focus on powerfully cleansing energy blocks.

zircon

With a relatively recent history of use in jewellery making, zircon ($ZrSiO_4$) has clear varieties that can be cut and polished to the

◁ Red coral is useful for balancing the emotions and for maintaining enthusiasm.

▽ Like many red crystals, red calcite takes its colour from iron atoms in the surrounding rock. It has a smooth, energizing effect.

brilliance of diamond. The yellow-red variety is traditionally known as 'jacinth' or 'hyacinth' and has always been popular in the Far East. Today zircon is important for its constituent, the rare metal zirconium –

a hard, heat-resistant metal that is used in industry as an anticorrosive and abrasive.

As a healing stone, zircon exhibits some of the useful spiritual properties of red stones. Like red crystals, such as red calcite,

red zircon warms the subtle bodies, helping to prevent the stagnant conditions of listlessness, melancholy and depression. Zircon can also help to ground and clarify spiritual experiences and will ease any tensions that may have arisen in the mind from psychic or visionary experiences. Zircon reminds us that vibrations of red energy are needed to maintain stability at all levels. Red energy provides fuel for our mental, emotional and physical wellbeing.

▽ Fire opal is one of the less common varieties. It is unmistakable, with a dense orange-red glow.

▽ Spinel usually forms small crystals with a characteristic double pyramid shape.

▽ Zircon crystals have a dull, red, metallic lustre and usually have clearly defined faces.

Rose quartz – healing the emotions

Rose quartz (SiO_2) is an important crystal for removing blocked emotional stress. It is generally considered to encourage love and harmony. It is true that the vibration of pink does reduce aggression and promote understanding and empathy, but it is a mistake to think that because of this wearing a rose quartz will make you feel happier.

emotional release

If there is suppression of barely controlled emotions, rose quartz will quite likely stir up a lot of turbulence. In such circumstances – and the majority of us have significant amounts of unresolved emotional stress – rose quartz can act like a safety valve, allowing a sudden release of emotional

▽ Emotions are complex and many layered things. You may need to use a variety of different stones to effectively release emotional stresses.

pressure. This can be an uncomfortable experience without understanding and guidance, and a little self-defeating if it creates further anxiety.

The guideline with rose quartz, as it should be with every crystal, is to explore the stone carefully and, if discomfort arises, change the approach. Our bodies are usually quite willing to correct imbalances gently, as long as they are provided with an appropriate stimulus. Stressful events tend to get frozen into repeating time-loops of memory in the body's muscles, as well as in the mind and emotional responses. Crystal healing is one of the most effective ways of allowing this trapped energy to release safely.

Emotional stress can become locked in any part of the body, and where it settles tension develops, restricting the local flow of energy. Starved of life-energy, these blocked areas become more susceptible to

CALMING THE EMOTIONS

The heart chakra is the centre of many of the body's energies and this is where we feel emotional hurt. This simple layout of stones will relax and ease any unexpected emotional upsets. It is also beneficial when used on a regular basis to prevent stress building up.

1 Place a small piece of rose quartz on the heart chakra in the centre of the chest.
2 Surround the rose quartz with four clear quartz crystals with points initially facing outwards. This will help to release stress.
3 Place a pointed citrine or smoky quartz over the second chakra below the navel, with its point downwards. This will have a gentle grounding and stabilizing effect and will also help to release any of the more long-term stresses that might be lodged in this centre.
4 Place an amethyst quartz crystal in the centre of the forehead. This will help to calm the mind and will encourage a degree of mental detachment from any emotional recall.

Lie in this calming layout for five to ten minutes or until you become aware of a feeling of relaxation and balance.

STRESS RELEASE POINTS
For the rapid, safe release of particular stresses, place small rose quartz stones on the slightly raised bumps to the sides of the forehead. You may need to tape the stones in place. Remembering the stressful event will begin the release process, which will be complete when you feel a change of emotion or a return of equilibrium. Placing a grounding stone by the feet and a balancing stone at the heart or solar plexus chakra may also help.

△ Rose quartz is useful to reduce any build-up of emotional stress and tension, and is also felt to encourage love and harmony.

▷ Keeping some rose quartz at your bedside can sometimes be effective as an aid to restful sleep.

illness. When the illness then causes pain and discomfort, the problem can be made worse by anger, irritation or disgust directed by the suffering person at their own affliction, as well as the draining emotions of fear, self-doubt and denial.

Local pain and inflammation can respond well to the placement of rose quartz as it calms and restores life-energy to the area. The addition of clear quartz points around the rose quartz, points directed away from the area, will also help remove imbalances.

Rhodonite and rhodocrosite – clearing and balancing

energizing and organizing

Two minerals rich in manganese form crystals of a beautiful pink. Rhodonite and rhodocrosite are both valuable in helping to bring balance to the emotions.

rhodonite

Named at the beginning of the 19th century after its colour – a rich rose pink – rhodonite $((Mn^{+2},Fe^{+2},Mg,Ca)SiO_3)$ is a hard, massive mineral, important in industry for its high manganese content. Rhodonite has become a popular semi-precious stone, especially the deep pink pieces patterned with dark brown or black oxides. It is cut as cabochons and carved into decorative ornaments.

Where the soft shades of translucent rose quartz may seem too gentle or soft, the balance of colours within rhodonite suggests a more robust and energetic character. The deep pink to magenta colours reflect the practical, down-to-earth vibration of caring

▽ Rhodonite combines the pink of emotional balance with the red and brown of a practical approach to life.

for oneself, having confidence and a sense of self-worth while remaining aware of the needs of others. The black or brown veins and patterns anchor rhodonite's energy into the solidity of the base chakra and through that to the earth itself. Because of its combination of colours, rhodonite works well at the base and sacral chakras. In emotional healing situations it complements and stabilizes the release initiated by rose quartz. Rhodonite will restore a sense of equilibrium without stifling the release processes that are underway. Always remember that grounding stones will quickly restore balance to a volatile emotional state.

Rhodonite can help to remove doubts about self-worth that prevent us from striving to achieve desired goals in life. A great deal of stress is created when personal ambitions are restrained or diverted. The entire structure of an individual's life energy can become distorted, leading to resentment, anger and aggression that may seem to have no apparent cause. Where

△ Wearing a pendant of rhodocrosite can help to encourage a more positive view of oneself.

these emotions are present rhodonite will help to divert the build-up of energy in positive and safe directions. Rhodonite used as a pendulum, wand or body sweep will identify the main areas of tension. Combined with blue stones, rhodonite will help us to find a way of achieving our ambitions.

rhodocrosite

This stone can sometimes be mistaken for its close relation rhodonite. Both are manganese ores, but rhodocrosite $(MnCO_3)$ often has additions of calcium, magnesium and iron. Whereas rhodonite is granular and opaque, rhodocrosite can be transparent or, more commonly, translucent. It usually forms in banded zones of pink, red, peach

▷ **Rhodocrosite crystallizes in shaded bands of pink, cream and peach. Large crystals form translucent deep salmon-pink rhomboids.**

and cream. Such a coloration lets rhodocrosite work on the base, sacral and solar plexus chakras, helping to blend their energies particularly where there is disruption due to emotional stress.

Poor self-worth and lack of self-confidence can manifest as problems in the digestive and reproductive systems. Anxiety creates tension in the stomach and pelvic areas, which can interfere with normal functioning. Particularly where there are emotional issues revolving around sexuality and fertility, rhodocrosite can help to ease negative perceptions.

In situations where there may be fear for one's safety, whether it is real or imagined, wearing a deep pink stone will help to reduce any anxiety and tension that themselves may create inappropriate reactions to those around you. Breathing through the stone, visualizing pink light around you, and allowing tensions to drain through the soles of the feet all help to achieve equanimity.

▽ **Rhodonite or Rhodocrosite can help to identify areas of emotional tension.**

STRESS RELEASE THROUGH BREATHING

Where obvious tension exists in the body, focusing the healing energy of pink light can help you to relax at a deep level. Use any kind of pink stone for this.

1 Place the stone on or near the area. Take a moment to let the awareness centre on that part of the body.

2 Now as you take a slow breath in, imagine that the air is focusing directly through the pink stone and right into the centre of the tension. Coloured by the pink stone, your breath will slowly begin to dissolve the pain and sorrow hidden there.

3 Each time you breathe out, feel the tensions melt and relax. Continue this for a minute or two, then lie quietly.

More pink stones

If ever there is any doubt about which crystal will resolve an imbalance, consider using a pink stone of some kind. This will always allow deep healing to take place. Pink stones not only help to clear emotional stress, they can also be powerfully protective, expressing as they do the energy of unconditional or universal love, perhaps more accurately called compassion. This quality of non-judgmental, unequivocal understanding and acceptance is a result of deep experience of the underlying unity of life. When this unity is felt there can be no fear, and without fear, aggression melts away.

kunzite

A pink variety of the mineral spodumene, (the green form of spodumene is hiddenite) kunzite ($LiAlSi_2O_6$) is coloured by manganese. Kunzite can be identified by the parallel striations that run the length of the crystal and by the fact that the colour is more intense when viewed down the cross section of its main axis. Gem-quality kunzite can be transparent and clear, while low-grade stones when tumbled are opaque lavender-pink. Kunzite is an excellent protector of the heart chakra and of the integrity of the emotions. Emotional energy is such a powerful force that sensitive people

▽ The clear brilliant pink of kunzite helps remove emotional debris from the heart and aura.

WAYS TO RELEASE NEGATIVITY

When you feel that you have acquired an uncomfortable or intrusive energy from outside yourself, or even if you are finding it difficult to let go of a certain emotional state, you can use kunzite to release negativity. In both these methods, the discordant energy becomes neutralized and harmless on passing through the crystalline structure of the 'exit' crystal. Make sure that all the stones you use are well cleansed before and after use to help them maintain their efficiency.

1 Sit quietly and simply observe the energy patterns you wish to get rid of. Then take a kunzite crystal in both hands and imagine all the unwanted energy, thoughts or emotions are draining out of your body through the stone as if it were a stream of water.
2 A variation of this can be to hold a kunzite or clear quartz in your left hand and another in your right hand. Visualize cleansing energy entering through the left and sweeping away unwanted energy through the right.

CLEARING UNWANTED ENERGY

This layout can be used when there is a feeling of energies 'stuck' within the personal aura. Emotions or memories may be repeating in an obsessive loop, or there may be a 'bad taste' from an unpleasant experience that you want to dispel.

1 Place a smoky quartz or a piece of kunzite between your feet pointing down and away from your body. Place a clear quartz or kunzite above the crown of the head pointing inwards. A third kunzite can be placed on the area where the negativity is most clearly felt.

2 Alternatively place the kunzite at each chakra point for a minute or two, starting with the brow and moving down the body to the sacral chakra.

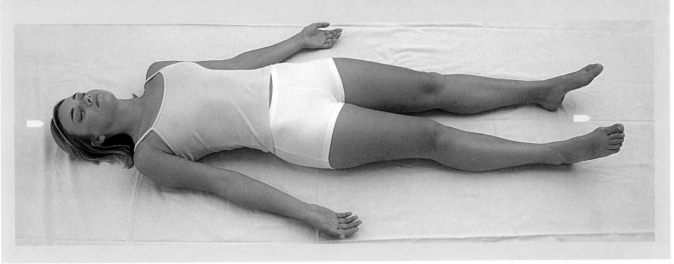

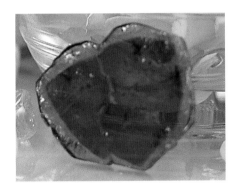

△ Rubellite is red tourmaline and is one of the most attractive of pink crystals.

▽ Lepidolite, or lithium mica, is a sparkly pink stone often found with rubellite embedded within it. It can support self-confidence and the clearing of emotional debris such as guilt.

can unwittingly pick up emotional debris from others. This can lead to unexpected mood swings and out-of-character behaviour. Placing or wearing a piece of kunzite by the heart for a while can help to sweep away this kind of negativity and any unwanted energy. Kunzite can be used as a release from any powerfully charged experience – such as a film, a song that gets stuck in the mind, or a hurtful remark.

If simply wearing a piece of kunzite is not sufficient, reinforce your intention with your imagination. This can be done in several ways, depending on what stones are available.

rubellite

One of the most beautiful pink crystals is red tourmaline, also called rubellite. Its colour ranges from a delicate pink to a rhubarb red. Usually the crystals are translucent, but occasionally they can be very dense and almost opaque.

With all types of tourmaline the density of colour changes slightly depending on the angle of view. This is caused by light rays becoming polarized as they pass through the crystal lattice. Like kunzite, rubellite has parallel striations along its length, which help it to act as an energy conduit. It also

△ The complex makeup of tourmaline means that it can contain many colours within a single crystal. 'Watermelon' combines red and green, a perfect heart chakra balancer.

has great strengthening and protecting effects on the heart chakra. Rubellite provides an excellent way to balance the emotions when there is either too much aggression (caused by fear or nervous irritation from external or internal imbalances) or too much passivity (caused by a poor level of self-esteem). Rubellite is sometimes found embedded in lepidolite, a stone which shares its qualities.

Often tourmaline combines shades of both red and green. This complex variety is called 'watermelon' tourmaline, and it holds the best combination of colours to balance the heart chakra and the emotions.

Carnelian and rutilated quartz – healing the wounds

Orange stones can often be effective repairers of the body, encouraging a rapid release of stress. Carnelian and rutilated quartz both encourage the body's own powers of regeneration.

carnelian

A variety of chalcedony, carnelian (SiO_2) is a microcrystalline quartz formed from the dissolving of other minerals containing silicates. Chalcedony does not have the crystalline lattice usually found in quartz. Instead, it is made up of closely packed fibres arranged in concentric layers or parallel bands. This stone gets its warm colour from the presence of iron oxides. It is often translucent, showing colours ranging from pale orange to a deep orange-red. As iron is a very common metal in the earth's crust, carnelian is found around the world. The

▷ **Carnelian is a warming stone that links well to the creative energy of the sacral chakra.**

ENERGY NET FOR HEALING THE ETHERIC BODY

Use this net regularly for five minutes at a time to help release trauma from deep in the body. It may sometimes bring old symptoms or pain to the surface before they can be completely removed. You will need six tumbled carnelians and an orange cloth to lie on.

1 Place one carnelian at the top of the head and one at either side of the body at the level of sacral chakra.
2 Place another stone between the legs at mid-calf level and another below it near the ankles. Place the sixth stone at the base of the throat.

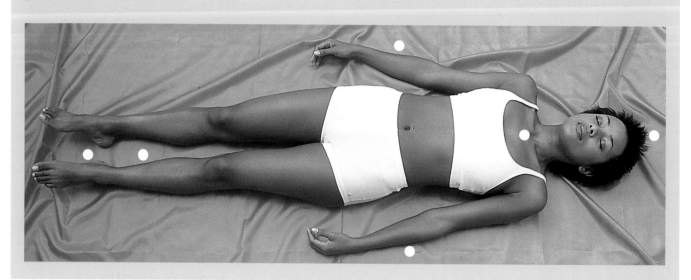

finest examples are used in jewellery – gem quality stones are traditionally known as 'sard'. Carnelian is one of the most useful stones for healing the etheric body when trauma and stress have accumulated to disturb physical functioning. Most will experience carnelian as a gentle soothing energy, though in some circumstances where it feels uncomfortable, the addition of some cooling green or blue stones may help.

rutilated quartz

This is clear or smoky quartz that contains fine thread-like crystals of rutile, titanium dioxide (TiO_2). Rutile is a metallic, needle-shaped crystal that can have a remarkable deep red colour. In quartz it is usually straw coloured – a lustrous gold to golden brown. Titanium is a non-corroding, extremely strong and light metal so it is no surprise that rutilated quartz can help to knit together and strengthen tissues that have been strained or damaged. Like many long,

△ Two pointed quartz crystals either side of the affected area, with the points facing each other, will diffuse a painful build-up of energy.

▽ Each crystal of rutilated quartz is different. Some have a few very long and fine threads of rutile running through them, which help repair nerve damage or connect energy pathways from different parts of the body. Other examples have tightly packed interwoven layers of rutile that might prove more effective in tissue repair.

TO EASE PAIN

Pain is a useful indicator of damaged tissue. Without that sensation we might not necessarily know that a problem exists. However, it is useful to be able to lower the levels of pain when they are very high. Pain is a concentration of energy, so by diffusing that energy the experience of pain can often be lessened. For repair of damaged physical tissue there must be a nourishing flow of energy to that area.

1 To ease the emotional stress of the situation, and to help repair be more rapid and complete, use pink, orange or yellow stones at the sacral chakra or solar plexus, with perhaps an addition of violet stones at the brow or crown chakra to establish calm.

2 To bring a cooling, quietening energy, place cool coloured stones, green, blue and violet, on or near a painful or inflamed area.

3 To speed the repair of tissues, such as pulled muscles and broken bones, place rutilated quartz on or around the affected area. This will encourage the torn tissues to rejoin and heal.

thin crystals, rutile is an excellent energy shifter and will help remove energy blocks. Its golden colour suggests that rutilated quartz can reorganize and integrate scattered energy fields.

Very often symptoms of physical pain can be eased when the energy flow within the meridian system is repaired. Detailed knowledge of these energy channels is not necessary – simply placing rutilated quartz or clear quartz crystal points at either side of the painful area, points facing each other, will often bring relief.

Use your hand to scan over the area so that you can feel the flow of energy. The appropriate direction of flow will feel different from any other direction. If needed, the flow can be encouraged by sweeping over the area with a hand-held crystal.

More orange healers

Copper and topaz share the ability to create a healing flow of energy through the body. For an even more gentle, clear orange energy, orange calcite is perhaps the coolest and most soothing of the orange stones.

These stones are ideal for helping internal emotional pressures that largely arise from unresolved situations or subtle, unnoticed sources in the environment, such as subsonic vibration or conflict with people around you. Pressure can also be caused by the wrong food or drink, ionization in the air prior to a storm, planetary influences and so on. Like a pressure cooker, energy begins to build up and, with no means of release, turbulence increases until an explosion of some kind restores the equilibrium. To avoid explosions, which can be a sudden, unwarranted loss of temper or could even develop into a nervous breakdown, you need to safely ground and release the unwanted energy.

RELEASING UNWANTED ENERGY

The following layout with orange stones can be used in acute cases of frustration or where there is a long term difficulty with a personal situation. The treatment helps to stimulate the creative flow of the sacral chakra and effectively grounds any excess energy through the feet.

Use any orange stones in this layout. Remain in position for 10-12 minutes.
1 Place one stone below the left foot.
2 Place another below the right foot.
3 Place a third stone a couple of centimetres below the navel.
4 Place a fourth stone a centimetre or so above the navel.

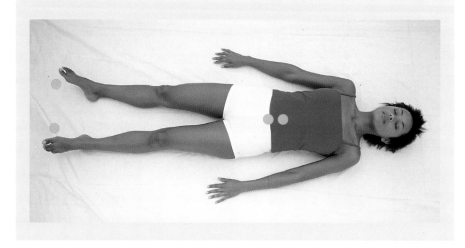

△ **Golden topaz is associated with qualities of leadership and self-assuredness. It can, however, be rather susceptible to absorbing energy, so needs regular cleansing if worn.**

topaz

Found in many degrees of colours from completely clear to green or blue, topaz $(Al_2SiO_4(F,OH)_2)$ is best known in its rich golden-yellow and orange-pink varieties. The colour is caused by traces of iron or chromium and may change in sunlight, becoming stronger or more faded.

In any of its colours topaz is good to use when the physical body is tense and emotions are volatile. It encourages the relaxation of rigid areas. Topaz will charge up any area it is focused on and can also be used to draw off excess or negative energy.

For a more grounded and gentler effect, tiger's eye (SiO_2 variety) can be used instead. This stone will also help the individual to integrate and become comfortable in challenging social situations.

▷ Water is able to hold the energy patterns of crystals placed in it.

copper

Metals can sometimes be found in a pure unmixed state in the earth, as nuggets or amalgamations known as native metals. All the precious and semi-precious metals have useful healing qualities, though sometimes they may be prohibitively expensive. Copper (Cu), a metallic red-orange that oxidizes to green, is a great conductor of energy. It is well known to be of benefit to rheumatic sufferers and its use can reduce inflammation of all sorts. Copper helps the flow of energy between all systems in the body and brings a stability and flexibility that protect against stress. When there is an energy build-up and an increasing sense of internal emotional or nervous pressure, copper can aid the flow of energy to safely release or ground it.

gem waters and essences

Releasing stress and trauma can be a long-term process. Using techniques to maintain the momentum between crystal healing sessions can speed the healing considerably. Gem waters and gem essences offer easy and effective ways of doing this and are simple to make and use. The energy patterns held in the water will only be released as and when the body requires.

▽ Emotional turbulence, over-emotional states or irritability can be eased with copper.

TO MAKE GEM WATER OR ESSENCE

When you are preparing to make a gem water or essence, choose a cleansed and washed sample of crystal. Members of the quartz family such as carnelian, and similar, harder minerals are ideal. Avoid very soft, water-soluble or potentially toxic minerals. Once you have made your gem water or essence, pour the water into a more permanent container such as an amber glass bottle and preserve it with alcohol or cider vinegar. Add a few drops to drinking water as required or rub on pulse points.

1 To make a gem water, place the crystal in a clean, plain glass or bowl and cover with spring water. Leave overnight and drink in the morning or take sips throughout the day.

2 To make a gem essence, place the stone in a clear glass bowl, cover it with spring water and put it in direct sunlight for at least two hours. This imprints the quality of the mineral on the water.

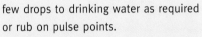

▽ Rub a drop of essence or gem water on pulse points for healing energy.

▽ Drink gem water within a day, while gem essences can be kept for much longer.

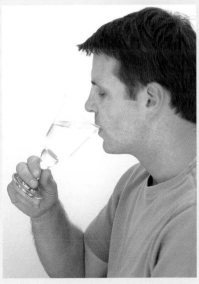

Citrine – sun and the mind

One of the rarer varieties of quartz, citrine (SiO_2) forms from recrystallized quartz solution where nearby oxidized iron impurities become included in the atomic structure. These impurities create the characteristic golden-yellow coloration of citrine. The finest quality of citrine is transparent lemon or golden yellow. More commonly, crystals are golden brown to orange-brown with milky white areas. Most citrine these days is made by gently heating poor quality amethyst, turning it golden. This process can also occur naturally in metamorphic environments.

Whatever its origin, citrine quartz is invaluable as a healing stone. The range of colours allows it to work as a grounding stone (browns), as a balancer of the sacral

▷ Citrine quartz is a translucent variety that shows a range of colours from brown to yellow.

CLARITY OF MIND LAYOUT

This energy net uses citrine to help clarity of mind, communication skills, adaptability and energy levels. It may quickly feel uncomfortable unless you really need the extra energy. Begin with short sessions of 5-6 minutes, and practise regularly, especially if you are studying. You will need three citrines, three clear quartz and a yellow cloth.

1 Place one citrine at the solar plexus, point down. Hold the other two citrines in the hands, points away from the body.
2 Place one clear quartz on the forehead with the point towards the top of the head. Tape the remaining clear quartz stones on the top of each foot, between the tendons of the second and third toes.

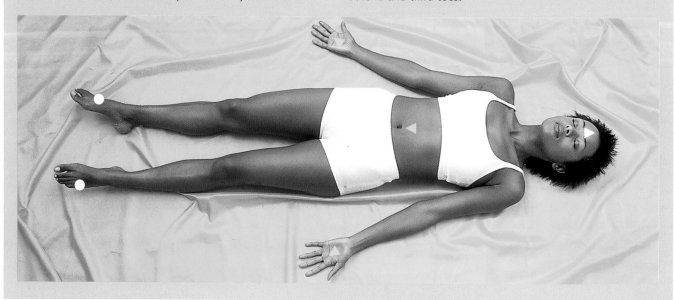

A CHAKRA GOAL BALANCING

This exercise can be used to help a friend or partner. A chakra goal balance uses crystals that will bring each of the chakras into balance and release the stresses related to the issue being looked at. Repeat the process regularly.

1 Encourage your friend or partner to share her problems and concerns with you, then together decide on a phrase or short sentence that sums up her intention.

2 Help her to intuitively select a stone for each chakra that will both balance the energy and also support the process of achieving the desired goal. When all the stones have been chosen, settle your friend in a comfortable position.

3 Place a stone on each chakra. Leave for 5 to ten minutes. Take away the stones, ground and centre her energies.

4 After the healing session give your friend a piece of citrine to take with her; this will help to keep confidence high and reduce any emotional turbulence the release may cause. When you repeat the process, new stones should be selected.

chakra (oranges) and as a support for the energies of the solar plexus chakra (yellows). Citrine is gently warming, soothing and integrating. Working in harmony with the solar plexus chakra, it is effective at increasing self-confidence and the achievement of personal goals. This crystal smoothes away areas of irritation and friction, creating more optimism and relaxation through the body, emotions and mind. Thought processes especially are helped with citrine – the grounding qualities prevent the build-up of anxieties, the oranges encourage a flow of creativity

and the bright yellows calm the digestive system. Citrine has a calming effect on the nervous system, bringing clearer thought and improved memory.

The solar plexus chakra, with which yellow stones work so effectively, is the seat of our sense of personal power. From this centre arise our beliefs or doubts in ourselves. From here, confidence or anxieties, optimism or fear modify all our beliefs and our behaviour. Working with yellow stones like citrine can be an effective way to strengthen the positive aspects and release the fears within the body.

goal balancing

Bad experiences, fear and anxiety often prevent us from achieving goals we would dearly love to reach. Removing the stresses that are linked to specific activities and personal behaviour patterns is one of the most rewarding techniques available to crystal healers.

There are many different ways of goal balancing. For example, with a pendulum it is possible to focus your intention on removing those stresses connected with the problem. The pendulum recognizes and releases only those related energy blocks.

More yellow stones

There is a crossover between crystals that work on the second and third chakras – the orange and yellow coloured stones. Citrine, topaz and tiger's eye, for example, will work well at either location depending on the exact shade of the stone.

The solar plexus chakra is especially important because it interfaces with many of the body's systems. The digestive system, the nervous system, the immune system, the brain and its memory function, all depend upon the solar plexus. The solar plexus is also the centre of emotional stability, the seat of personal power, hope and optimism.

Crystal healing is one of the best ways to release the tension that affects the solar plexus, causing stomach problems. Yellow stones help to support positivity and access reserves of personal initiative.

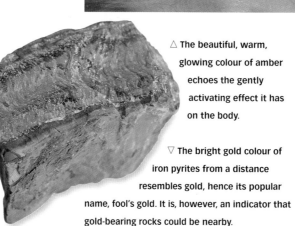

▷ Tiger's eye can be used at the base, sacral and solar plexus chakras, depending on the precise mix of colour in each stone.

▽ Nuggets of pure gold are rare. A very small piece of gold could be attached to a slab of clear quartz to enable its use in crystal healing sessions.

△ The beautiful, warm, glowing colour of amber echoes the gently activating effect it has on the body.

▽ The bright gold colour of iron pyrites from a distance resembles gold, hence its popular name, fool's gold. It is, however, an indicator that gold-bearing rocks could be nearby.

amber

Not strictly a mineral or a crystal, amber ($C_{10}H_{16}O+H_2S$) is fossilized tree resin more than four million years old. It can be brown, orange, yellow, green or red, perfectly clear or contain bits of debris from when it oozed from the bark of ancient pine trees. Amber containing whole preserved insects tends to be highly valued and is often imitated with plastic or resin. It can be worked very easily with abrasive papers and reheated to melt small fragments together into larger pieces, producing so-called Russian amber.

Amber is a soothing stone that is useful for correcting imbalances in the nervous system, or when there is a need for gentle activation and energizing. Amber can be helpful for detoxification and reduces confusion and anxiety.

iron pyrites

With its high sulphur content, iron pyrites (FeS_2) can have beneficial effects on the digestive system, helping with the elimination of toxins. More commonly known as fool's gold, pyrites forms brilliant

▷ Gold jewellery will have some beneficial effects on the energies of the body.

▽ Yellow coloured stones help to reduce tension in the solar plexus and encourage relaxation and positive attitudes.

golden metallic crystals, often perfect cubes. As an iron ore, it is gently grounding, helping recovery from flights of anxiety and other emotionally charged imaginings that contribute to depression and frustration. If anxiety is a factor in digestive problems, pyrites can help reduce tension.

other yellow stones

A commonly occurring native metal, though usually in quantities so small as to be uneconomical to retrieve, gold has been sought after and treasured since the Stone

▽ Sunstone is a variety of feldspar with a yellow-orange colour and a brilliant play of light. It is of the same family as moonstone.

Age. Forming from gold-bearing rocks or in hot water solution it is usually found near to granite rock masses and in quartz veins. As these erode the grains of gold are deposited in river gravels.

Gold rarely crystallizes but forms thin plates, wires and grains. Nuggets are very uncommon. Gold is not often used in crystal healing, simply because natural examples large enough to be practical are rare. Small flakes of gold can be found in mineralogical shops boxed for display.

Like the other elemental metals, silver and copper, gold is a great conductor of energy, helping to harmonize many of the different levels within the body. Creating easy energy flow, gold is helpful in releasing stress from the nervous system, increasing the efficiency of the brain and the ability to repair damaged tissues. The immune system is strengthened by gold's positive effect on the heart chakra and thymus gland. In the absence of a piece of native gold, a clean piece of 24 carat jewellery can be used.

Stones such as fluorite, feldspar, beryl and tourmaline all have yellow varieties that can play a part in rebalancing the solar plexus chakra. Those stones with a warm orange-yellow work best with the digestive system and will be relaxing. The stones with a more lemon yellow colour will be effective in clearing the mind and nervous system, encouraging clarity and mental alertness.

Balance and Peace:
green and blue stones

Crystals with the cooler colours of
blue and green all tend to encourage
a sense of balanced calm and a quality
of peacefulness. These crystals work
well with the energies of the heart and
throat chakras.

Green stones – balancing the heart

There are a great many minerals and crystals with a green coloration. All work very well to balance the heart chakra energies and introduce stabilizing and calming influences.

green aventurine

A member of the quartz family, green aventurine (SiO_2) is one of the best overall balancing stones for the heart, because it acts without creating any turbulence or sudden release. Aventurine forms when quartz is subjected to heat and pressure, causing it to melt and resolidify, usually as large slabs, with inclusions of other minerals. It is these inclusions that give aventurine its colour. Green aventurine resembles green jasper but contains fuschite mica or sparkling fragments of haematite and pyrite, which catch the light and make it easy to distinguish from other similar stones. The inclusions have a slight grounding effect that increases the stabilizing qualities of the stone.

▽ Aventurine is a massive form of quartz that can be found in a range of colours from emerald to very pale green.

△ Bloodstone of the finest quality is a dark green with bright red spots and splashes. It can also contain areas of grey, yellow and orange.

bloodstone

Another green member of the quartz family, bloodstone (SiO_2) is well known for its beneficial effects on the heart and circulation. In the past it was believed to be effective in staunching wounds and soldiers

△ Verdelite can be distinguished from similar coloured stones because, like all tourmalines, the colour alters slightly with the angle of viewing.

used to carry a piece with them into battle. Heliotrope, as bloodstone is also called, is a type of chalcedony with the same structure as jasper. The green colour is caused by small crystals of actinolite, while the prominent bright red spots and streaks derive from iron oxides that were present as the solution crystallized. With a combination of red and green, bloodstone can work with both the base and heart chakras, bringing either a sufficient energy or a sufficient calmness.

verdelite

Green tourmaline ($Na(Mg,Fe,Li,Mn,Al)_3Al_6(BO_3)Si_6O_{18}(OH,F)_4$) is also known as verdelite. The green colour, which can vary from very light to almost black, is brought about by higher than usual amounts of sodium in the structure of the stone.

All tourmalines help to re-align the physical structures of the body and our connection to the energies of the planet. Its green colour attunes verdelite more to the heart chakra and to a relationship with the natural world. Like many green minerals, verdelite increases our receptivity allowing greater harmony with the surroundings.

BALANCING THE HEART'S ENERGIES

The heart is the balance point for our entire energy system. Creating balance and stability in the heart makes it easier for other imbalances elsewhere to be corrected. Balancing the heart brings a life-supporting calm inside us, and an ability to relate positively to the world around us. The following layout of crystals helps to stabilize all the energies of the heart.

Beneath the heart chakra is another small energy centre that is particularly concerned with holding and bringing to fruition our most cherished wishes and desires. A Herkimer diamond placed just under the heart (pictured right) will help access this energy, bringing a sense of clarity and direction when there is confusion.

1 For the layout shown below, first place a small rose quartz crystal at the centre of the chest.

2 Then take four green tourmalines, and make a cross along the axis of the body around the rose quartz. Clear quartz can be used here if tourmalines are unavailable. It is important that, if the stones have natural points, these are all placed so that they are facing outwards.

3 Between the four tourmalines make a second diagonal cross using smoky quartz crystals. Again, if these have natural points they should face outwards. This pattern will release stress from the heart while balancing and grounding its energies. The outward pointing stones ensure that a relaxing calm is established. Stay in this heart layout for five to ten minutes. Use grounding stones if necessary afterwards.

4 For a variation of this layout, if you want to bring full potential closer within your reach, then you can add a Herkimer diamond underneath the layout.

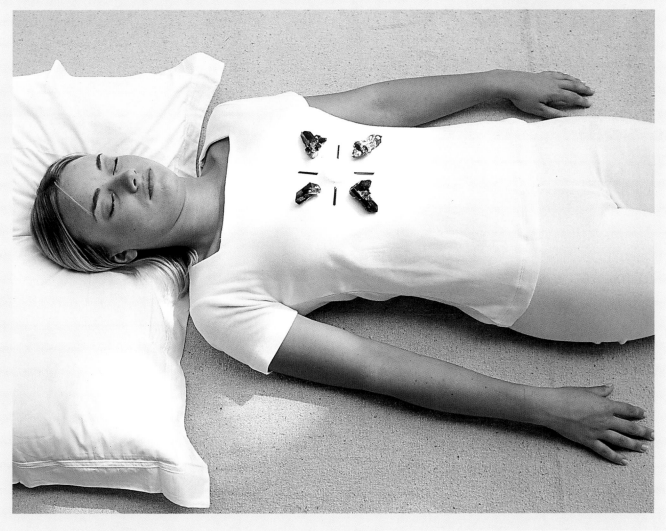

Green crystals and the space of nature

Green is the colour of nature, the energy of expansion and space. The heart chakra establishes our own inner space and our relationship to everything in the world around us. Green stones and crystals can help to create the fine balance that we need in order to live harmoniously with the world without suppressing our own desires. Green crystals can also help to break down some of the barriers that keep us feeling trapped within our circumstances and the limits of our abilities.

moss agate

Common symptoms of feeling trapped are tightness in the chest and breathing difficulties. Moss agate, a form of chalcedony, with coloured inclusions resembling trees, ferns or moss, can help to relieve the tensions that underlie these problems. Within the translucent or transparent quartz, which usually has a blue or yellow tinge, crystal growths of manganese oxides, hornblende or iron in various shades of green and brown suggest the ability to grow and expand. The inclusions often look like the fine structures within the lungs, suggesting freedom to breathe. Moss agate encourages a sense of increased confidence and optimism, allowing a much greater relationship with the world of nature.

jade

By connecting us to our physical instincts and earth energies, jade ($NaAlSi_2O_6$) increases the sense of belonging. Thus jade is an antidote to over-intellectual spiritualism – it calms the arrogance that sees the physical world as inferior to the flights of fancy the mind can conjure up.

emerald

This stone is a gem-quality green variety of the mineral beryl ($Be_3Al_2Si_6O_{18}$). It balances the heart, speeds up detoxification and brings calm by removing hidden fears. Like many green stones, emerald can be a helpful aid to meditation.

healing the garden

Green stones have a natural affinity with growing plants and they can be used to heal the energies of a garden. Simply place stones where you feel extra help is needed. Walk round your garden, allowing yourself to be receptive to energy changes. You will almost certainly be drawn to spots that feel dull or heavy in some way. This process is similar to scanning a body and is corrected in the same way by the placement of appropriate stones. Minerals with a significant copper content, such as turquoise, malachite and chrysocolla can all encourage plant growth.

△ **Green stones make a space calm and restful for contemplation and meditation.**

making space

Healing the heart can never truly be accomplished if whenever we reduce stress, we return immediately to a hectic and stressful life. For anything to grow, space is needed. If we wish to get more from life, sometimes it is necessary to do less instead of trying to cram more things in.

▽ **Moss agate can be a useful calming stone for feelings of confinement and confusion.**

▽ **Jade has been widely used for rituals and is linked to ancestor spirits and the gods.**

▽ **Emerald of gem-quality is rare and expensive but impure pieces work in healing just as well.**

A SMALL CALM SPACE

Finding a few minutes once a day to be silent in your own company will help you to see opportunities and new solutions that would improve the quality of your life. Crystals can help to bring balance into our energy systems but it is up to us to maintain and build upon that state of balance.

Use some green stones to bring some of the qualities of nature into your home. Set a small space aside in a corner or on a table. Keep it clear of everyday clutter, and arrange some of your favourite green stones there, together with a beautiful plant and a candle, or other items that help you feel calm and relaxed.

1 Take two minutes a day to sit and look at the stones. Sit comfortably in front of them, light the candle or burn some incense.

2 Take up one or two of the stones and hold them in your hands, close your eyes and relax. You are making space in your mind, your emotions and your life for new things to enter.

3 Open your eyes to look again at the stones and then close them again and think of the space you are creating in your mind. Repeat if you wish.

4 When you have finished, return the stones to their place.

▽ ▷ **The energy of any room in the home can be enlivened by having a small quiet space somewhere within it**.

Personal space – individual growth

Green stones strengthen the main quality of the heart chakra, which is to grow and expand in a harmonious manner in such a way as to fulfil the individual's core needs. Personal space and freedom to be oneself are essential for wellbeing and health. We can use crystals to help us achieve our goals in life, both by giving us quiet in order to see things more clearly and by encouraging the growth of qualities we need.

Before goals can be reached, it is necessary to clarify as much as possible what those goals are. A reminder of your aim keeps your attention focused in the right direction without becoming obsessive. Set aside a space that can be dedicated to your wishes. Have a representation of your goal; a picture, photograph or phrase. For example, if the goal is to pass your driving test, a picture of a car can be the centrepiece. Then choose crystals to encourage qualities that are needed for you to succeed. Encourage optimism and clarity with yellow crystals, calm with green stones, ability to learn with blue, co-ordination with violet. A clear quartz crystal can reinforce your intention if it is programmed.

▽ **This space is dedicated to a wish for personal control and confidence. The yellow crystals will help to encourage optimism and reduce anxiety.**

GREEN BREATHING

This exercise easily creates a meditative state. Using a green crystal as a focus of attention naturally calms the mind and acts as a support to the entire process. Sit in a comfortable position and take a minute to settle yourself. Have a green stone in front of you – the type is not important.

1 Look at the stone, letting your eyes rest on it gently. Keep looking at the stone and let your mind be aware of your breathing.

2 After a few minutes, close your eyes and imagine you are breathing in the colour green. If you get distracted, open your eyes and gaze at the stone for a while longer, then close your eyes and breathe in the colour again.

3 When you are ready, put the stone aside and relax for a minute before returning to normal activity.

▷ Exposing a clear quartz crystal to a range of coloured lights is an effective way of programming it, or modifying its energy.

programming a crystal

To direct a crystal's energy towards a specific, clearly defined goal you need to programme it. This will always be most effective when your intention matches the natural quality of the crystal. Programming a blue crystal to radiate red energy is possible, for example, but will go against the flow of energy that crystal possesses. Always get to know a crystal well before you consider modifying its function with programming. Remember that a crystal that has always been used for its healing energy will always be better suited to healing rather than being used as a meditation stone. A meditation crystal will come to enhance and amplify the energies of the meditator each time it is used, and so will be less useful as a healing stone.

There are two ways to programme a crystal. The first way is by exposure to a type of energy, such as a light source. A clear quartz that is exposed for a prolonged amount of time to red light, for example, will after a while begin to resonate to that red frequency.

The second programming technique is to redirect the stone's energy through strong intention and affirmation. Hold the stone in your hands, or to your heart or brow, and project your intention into the centre of the crystal. Repeat this process several times until you intuitively feel that the crystal can now hold and broadcast the thought or intention. For sucessful programming, it is important that the intention you project is as clear and precise as possible. Vague or muddled desires bring vague results.

Once it is programmed, place the crystal carefully in a space where it can be seen, to remind you of your goals.

To remove the programming repeat the process with the intention that the stone reverts to its normal state. Cleanse the crystal and thank it for its help.

GREEN HEART
This exercise will calm the heart.
1 Put a green stone at your heart. Hold a clear quartz crystal in your left hand, point inwards. Hold another clear quartz in your right hand, point outwards, away from the body.
2 Visualize a flow of energy from your left hand to your heart and from your heart to your right hand and out of your body. Feel calm energy filling you and tension draining away.
3 Change the quartz points around so the flow moves in the other direction. Repeat the process.
4 After five minutes put down the quartz points and experience the calm green energy at the heart chakra. If there is somewhere else that is in pain or in need of extra calming energy, put the green stone there, instead of at the heart.

Expansion into the beyond – stones from space

Tons of dust land on the planet from space every year but it is rare to find larger fragments, even though meteorites have crashed into the earth since its creation. Metallic meteorites consisting mainly of iron and nickel are more common than rocky meteorites that have a composition similar to igneous rock. Many meteorites are thought to be the remnants of a planet that once orbited between Mars and Jupiter, a space now occupied by the asteroid belt.

tektites

Even more mysterious than meteorites are tektites, a group of minerals found scattered around the globe whose exact origins are unknown. Tektites may be glassy meteorites but it is more likely that they formed millions of years ago when large meteorites struck the earth, melting rock in huge explosions of energy. The strange shapes of tektites are evocative of such cataclysmic events. Very often they have pitted, rippled or cratered surfaces and form pebble, teardrop or elongated extruded fragments. They are usually black-brown. In one area in the Czech Republic tektites are a brilliant green, and there they are called moldavites.

moldavites

These are much sought-after, even though they are rarely found in large pieces. Moldavite is an excellent amplifying stone,

▷ **Meteorites remind us of the vastness of the universe and the possibilities of the unknown.**

MOLDAVITE NET

If you are lucky enough to have nine moldavite pieces you can try the following crystal net. This energy net will help expand awareness beyond its normal physical limitations. It will help connect you to the energy of the earth, and through its core energy out into the wider universe. This layout will help relax tensions in the chest, easing feelings of constriction and confusion. It will also help clarify your goals and directions in life. Moldavite can give a powerful and sometimes disorientating experience. Make sure you spend no longer than ten minutes in this net and ground yourself thoroughly when finished.

1 On either side of the body between the head and solar plexus put three moldavites, evenly spaced.

2 Position another moldavite midway between and below your feet.

3 Place one above the top of your head.

4 The last moldavite goes on the brow chakra in the centre of the forehead.

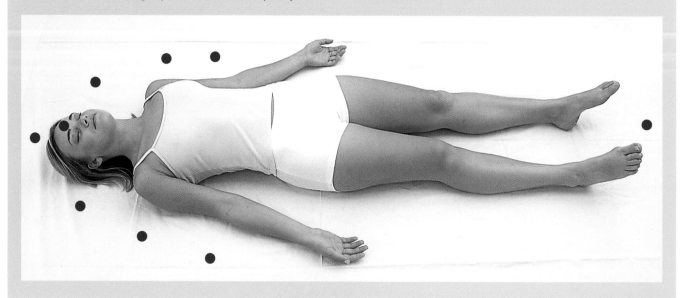

EXPLORING MOLDAVITE

The energy of moldavite definitely seems to be unearthly at times, as befits a stone created from the meeting of earth and outer space. Comfortable exploration of moldavite's potential can be helped with this layout.

1 Use eight pieces of amethyst or eight pieces of clear quartz. If they have terminations, place these so they are facing inwards towards the body.

2 Once these are in place, place the moldavite on your heart, throat or brow chakra. Experiment with the moldavite on different chakras to see how your experiences alter.

3 After a maximum of ten minutes remove the moldavite and replace it with a grounding stone, such as haematite or black tourmaline. Another grounding stone can be added near the feet if necessary.

4 When you are ready, remove all the stones and relax for at least five minutes before resuming normal activities.

enhancing the properties of other stones placed with it. It usually feels expansive and enlivening and it may cause sensations of movement or sudden changes of energy and awareness, such as heat or flashes of imagery across the mind. It is well worth sitting for a time with a piece of moldavite and just allowing these tides of energy to come and go. If you wish to explore more deeply, place a piece of moldavite at your heart, throat or brow chakra and surround your body with clear quartz or amethyst. Keep a good grounding stone nearby for when you have finished. Do not place too much meaning on your experiences. Simply accept.

When exploring the qualities of crystals in this way remember to make notes of your experiences afterwards. Over time certain themes and types of imagery will emerge and these may suggest how the crystal is interacting with your own energy systems.

With stone such as moldavite there can be a powerful amplifying effect. This makes them useful in the exploration of other sorts of crystal. Green stones in general, and moldavite in particular, seem to enhance our natural sensitivity and psychic skills, particularly if we have learned the value of entering a quiet, receptive, calm state on a regular basis.

◁ **Moldavite has a characteristic bottle-green colour and a rippled or pitted surface pattern**.

▷ **Although attractive in its natural shapes, moldavite is also used in jewellery**.

Turquoise and aquamarine – joy and the immune system

Activating and strengthening the body's own defences naturally improves quality of life, bringing an increased sense of optimism and happiness. Both turquoise and aquamarine can be used for this purpose. Happiness is one of the greatest antibiotics available to us. It rapidly creates balance in the blood chemistry and hormones, releasing stress and flushing out damaging toxins.

turquoise

A hydrated basic phosphate of aluminium and copper, turquoise ($CuAl_6(PO_4)_4(OH)_8.4H_2O$) is of medium hardness, and the colour – which varies – can alter when exposed to light or chemicals. Despite its lack of stability it has been used throughout the world as an important gemstone.

In North American Indian traditions, in China and Tibet, as well as in Europe, turquoise has a reputation for protection. There is a belief that the stone will become paler when its owner is in danger. Certainly it will react to chemicals secreted from the skin as well as to oils or perfumes being worn. Because of its susceptibility, the colour of turquoise is often stabilized with wax or resin. In the southwestern United States, turquoise was often powdered and presented

△ Turquoise is one of the most universal and oldest of gemstone amulets worn for protection.

▽ Turquoise is a soft mineral. Often in jewellery making it is crushed to a powder and mixed with resin, to make a more robust-coloured stone.

INCREASING LIFE ENERGY
The thymus gland is located between the heart and throat chakras. It is an important organ of the immune system and at energetic levels regulates the amount of life-energy, or *prana*, within the body. All turquoise-coloured stones placed around this area will help to regulate and balance the thymus.

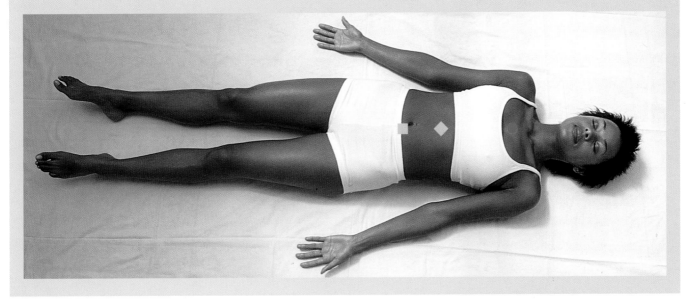
◁ Aquamarine is so-named from its colour resembling the sea. It was once prized as a protection from shipwreck.

as an offering to the spirits. In Central and South America it was used to decorate offerings to the gods. The delicate sky-blue tones suggest its affinity to the heavens – sky that has fallen to earth.

The colour of turquoise has a strengthening and supporting effect on the thymus gland, which is located just below the throat where the collarbones meet. This gland is one of the main organs of the immune system. In complementary medicine, it is of vital importance to the levels of life-energy available in the body.

Turquoise encourages the functions of this gland and so increases available energy, protecting the body from negativity.

aquamarine

Blue-green in colour, aquamarine ($Be_3Al_2Si_6O_{18}$) is a variety of the mineral beryl, which can form very large crystals up to several metres long. Many of the finest crystals are found in Brazil, and it is a good source of the light metal beryllium, which is used in alloys. Aquamarine is excellent for energizing the immune system and is useful in the recovery from debilitating illnesses, where it provides an energy boost, helping the body to get rid of the underlying causes of disease. Whereas turquoise is an absorbing stone with gentle actions, aquamarine can be stimulating and purifying. Occasionally it may appear to exacerbate symptoms as they are lifted from the subtle bodies. If this occurs, use it with a stone that will ease the process such as kyanite or selenite.

An important quality of the thymus, located midway between the heart and throat, is the expression of uniqueness. Repressing our natural qualities suppresses life-energy, leading to stress and susceptibility to illness. If you are in a situation where you cannot be yourself, use aquamarine to find a positive way to express your individuality. Aquamarine can help clear localized areas of imbalance and dulled energy. Placing it on or near an infected or inflamed area will help to release the difficulties that hamper the body's defence systems.

TURQUOISE LAYOUT

Use this layout when healing energies are required or there is a lack of self-confidence. Turquoise stimulates the natural protective energies of the body, citrine reduces fear and balances the body's functions.

1 Place a turquoise just below the collarbones.
2 Place a bright yellow citrine at the solar plexus.
3 Place a rose quartz at the navel to calm and stabilize the emotions.

Amazonite and chrysocolla – self-expression and creativity

Turquoise stones help to combine and harmonize the energies of the heart and throat chakras, easing the flow of personal expression and individuality. Amazonite and chrysocolla improve communication on many different levels.

amazonite

A variety of the common mineral feldspar, amazonite ($KAlSi_3O_8$) has been used for centuries in jewellery and ornamentation because of its fine blue-green colour. Characteristic to amazonite is a streaky parallel patterning of different shadings, caused by the presence of lead, the impurity of which creates the intense colour.

Like turquoise, amazonite can sometimes be more blue and sometimes more green in colour, and this makes it useful both at the heart chakra and the throat chakra – but of special value for the thymus gland midway between them both.

Amazonite is particularly effective at activating the qualities of self-expression,

confidence, leadership and communication. Like many green and turquoise stones, amazonite may also help to enhance psychic skills, in particular the ability to receive images from the past. This ability is known as 'far memory'. The images received often relate to, or are symbolic of, current preoccupations and parallel or reflect the current goals of the viewer. Whether these

△ **Amazonite often shows streaks of different greens along its central axis. It forms clearly defined block-like crystals.**

far memories are actually past life information, or come from another subconscious source, their impressions can be useful in encouraging us to locate, order and pursue our unique path in life.

AMAZONITE NET

An energy net of six pieces of amazonite can be used to release skills hidden deep within our genetic memory. It can also help the recall of distant personal memories, throwing light on repeating patterns of behaviour. This helps to clarify what prevents us from achieving our goals time and again, so that steps can be taken to remove hidden blocks. Place six amazonites evenly around the body: one above the head, one below the feet and two at either side. Allow five to ten minutes for a session.

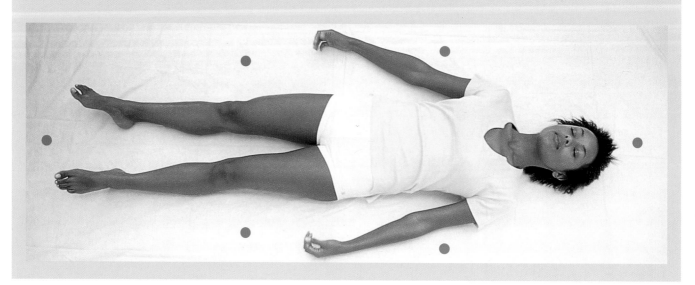

▷ Those who work creatively may benefit from chrysocolla, as it releases tension in the upper body and helps the flow of creative expression.

▽ Its effects on the thoracic cavity and throat make chrysocolla of benefit to singers.

chrysocolla

A delicate and very beautiful mineral, chrysocolla $((Cu,Al_2)H_2Si_2O_5(OH)_4 \cdot nH_2O)$ is formed from solutions of copper, silica and water. Because it occurs near copper deposits it can be found intermixed with other copper-rich minerals such as turquoise, azurite, malachite and cuprite. Chrysocolla often intergrows with quartz, which makes it slightly more durable,

though still soft. In this form it is called gem silica. A variety of chrysocolla mixed equally with turquoise and azurite-malachite has a deeper, even blue-green colour and is known as Eilat stone. This variety is named for the region on the Sinai Peninsula where it was mined in the time of King Solomon.

Chrysocolla helps to balance the whole region of the chest, lungs, throat and neck. It cools and calms inflamed areas, stimulating

the immune system and quietening the mind. The mix of greens and blues acts on the heart and throat chakras, reaching up to the deeper blue of the brow chakra and the related minor chakra at the base of the skull, the medulla oblongata. This small energy point is important for regulating and directing psychic information and energy from other levels of existence. It clears away blockages in the emotions and belief systems, which cause confusion and failure.

Placing a piece of chrysocolla at the heart or throat, at the base of the skull or in the centre of the forehead can create a rearrangement of energies that results in a clearer view of issues. For particular problems, begin with a clear intention or a situation you wish to understand better. Focus clearly for a moment on that thought and then relax. The chrysocolla will help to bring resolutions to your conscious mind.

At a physical level, chrysocolla encourages relaxation and balance, allowing the green energies of the heart, with all its strength of feeling, to be manifested and expressed through the blue energies of the throat chakra and the voice.

◁ Chrysocolla can have strong areas of green next to rich, deep turquoise and blue. Its irregular and flaky appearance in natural form helps to identify it from other similarly coloured minerals.

Blue lace agate and celestite – touching the clouds

Light blue stones, such as blue lace agate and celestite, are used to introduce a calming influence in situations where cool, peaceful energy is required.

blue lace agate

This is one of the most striking varieties of quartz. The rich blue bands in blue lace agate (SiO_2) are created by larger quartz crystals intergrowing through chalcedony, which originally seeped as solution into cavities within volcanic rock. This natural blue agate is not commonly found, so it tends to be rather more expensive than other agates. Because of its microscopic structure, all agate is very porous and will take up dyes easily. Dyed agate is relatively easy to identify as all its bands are shades of one colour, whereas natural samples have some variation created by the different impurities in the surrounding rocks where they crystallize.

Few crystals have the soft, gentle energy of lace agate. It can be used anywhere that needs calming and cooling. Blue stones encourage the flow of energy and have a natural affinity with the throat chakra, our

means of communication and expression. When the flow of communication is stifled, internal pressure builds up. Unexpressed, this energy can become resentment, anger and aggression; unable to flow, the blue vibration becomes red energy that will eventually explode. Blue stones can help to ease the pressure and release the energy.

△ All agates are a microcrystalline quartz in massive form only, though sometimes small crystals can be seen within the layers.

▽ A feeling of pressure is often felt at the throat when emotional stress is being released. A piece of blue lace agate placed at the base of the throat will quickly ease and release the energy.

▽ When polished, blue lace agate reveals undulating bands of blues and milky greys.

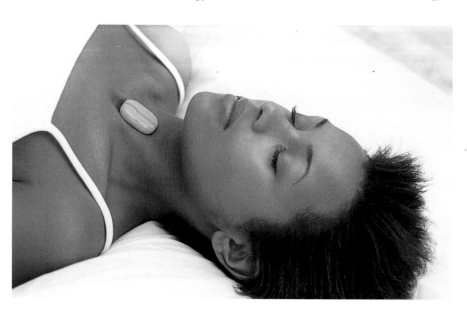

celestite

Also known as celestine, celestite ($SrSO_4$) is a soft blue or grey mineral that has been used for centuries as an ingredient in fireworks and rescue flares. The strontium content burns with a bright crimson flame.

The finest celestite crystals come from Madagascar and are a beautiful sky-blue colour, hence the mineral name. Celestite has an uplifting, calming and expansive quality, making it good for contemplation and meditation. It is effective at lifting heavy moods and sadness as well as balancing the throat chakra. The ethereal quality of celestite crystals often helps the mind to travel beyond its normal perspective, promoting inspiration and intuitive leaps.

▷ **Celestite is easily damaged as it is very soft, so keep it away from harder stones in a collection.**

ETHER NET

Using an energy net with seven small clusters of celestite and a white cloth will help you tune into spiritual states as well as encouraging communication skills and artistic creativity. Ether is the fifth element, the element of space. Within its fine substance are all the possibilities of creation. Lying in this energy net can provide a deep rest from the cares of the world, and an effective way to lighten heavy emotional burdens. It can also help dissolve negative patterns that have become attached to the auric field.

Lay out the seven clusters on the white cloth, one above the head, one at either side of the feet and the others evenly spaced between. Lie in the net for five to ten minutes.

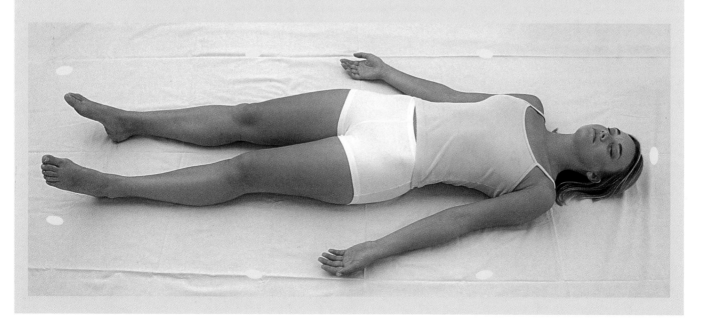

Healing and Beyond:
indigo and violet stones

With deeper blue and violet crystals
the potential for change and growth
of awareness greatly increases as our
inherent abilities and buried talents
emerge to enrich our lives. These stones
attune to the brow and crown chakras.

Indigo stones – lapis lazuli and sodalite

There are many deep blue minerals available, all of which can help us to regain a state of quiet peaceful awareness, in which we become more receptive to all sorts of information and communication.

lapis lazuli

A rare gemstone that has always been highly prized, lapis lazuli $(Na,Ca)_8(Al.Si)_{12}O_{24}(S,SO_4)$ forms only where limestone comes into contact with calcite and pyrites. Metamorphic conditions produce a new mineral, lazurite, which has an intense blue coloration. Lapis lazuli is a rock comprising several minerals: lazurite embedded in calcite and pyrites. Afghanistan has always been the best source.

▽ **The rich blues of lapis lazuli were once ground to a fine powder and used as pigment.**

Lapis lazuli works well with the whole area of the upper chest, throat and head. It can be very quietening initially, but this is often the prelude to deep cleansing at many different levels. Lapis can help those who are shy or introverted to communicate and express themselves. It can also benefit those who project their voices, such as teachers, singers and sales personnel.

Like other deep blue and indigo stones, lapis lazuli attunes to the throat and brow chakras and enlivens communication, the processes of thought and memory. The energy of lapis lazuli is not comfortable for everyone, provoking detachment and floating into uncharted depths. This apparent emptiness, when patiently absorbed, reveals a wealth of information and solutions to problems. It can also reveal past errors and bring up unresolved fears.

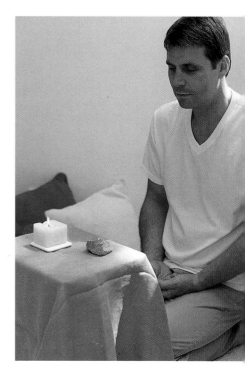

△ **The peaceful, calm presence of lapis lazuli brings a lively silence to a meditation room and aids thought processes.**

sodalite

This mineral can be easily confused in appearance with lapis lazuli. Indeed, sodalite $(Na_4Al_3Si_3O_{12}Cl)$ can often be found as one of the minerals making up lapis. The main differences are a slight variation of blue – lapis is more brilliant, sodalite darker. Lapis contains specks of golden iron pyrites and has a speckling of different colours, while sodalite has thin veins of white running through it. Sodalite is named from its high sodium content. It is a useful stone for the brow chakra. It can be less penetrating in its energy than lapis lazuli, but can help nevertheless to access fine levels of intuitive knowledge and promote understanding of ideas and concepts. It is therefore a useful stone for the student and the philosopher.

Physically sodalite will, like all dark blue stones, have a sedating and quietening effect on overactive systems, particularly the nervous system and the lymphatic system,

◁ **A flow of fine levels of information is suggested by the web-like structure and veins of colours within sodalite.**

▽**Sodalite promotes understanding and is helpful placed close by when studying.**

which is suggested by the web of fine white veins throughout the stone. This visual characteristic also reflects the ability of sodalite to strengthen communication, particularly in groups.

Indigo stones should be used sparingly with those suffering from depressive states as the colour can exaggerate the condition. Choose activating, warm coloured stones to encourage optimism and dynamism.

LAYOUT FOR INCREASING EASE

Sometimes there is a feeling of unease, of things being not quite right without any apparent symptoms of illness or upset in your life. Because of its potent cleansing energy lapis lazuli can be used to alleviate this in a simple procedure that can be remarkably powerful.

1 Place a clear quartz, point upwards, above the crown of the head. Place a smoky quartz, point down, between the feet.
2 At the centre of the brow place a piece of lapis lazuli. Remain in the layout for five to ten minutes and repeat for a few days if necessary.

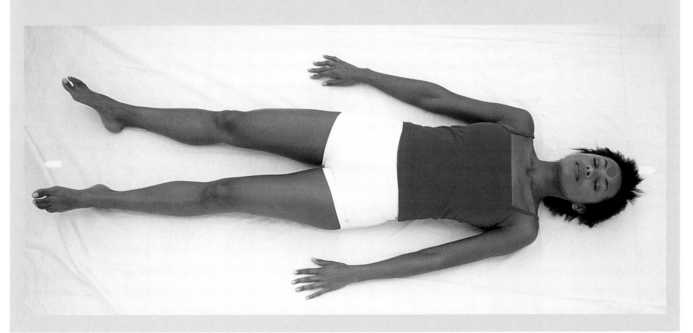

More blue stones – intuition

Becoming a good crystal healer requires a degree of knowledge about tools and techniques, but most of all it is necessary to have confidence in your own intuitive abilities. Crystals can be described only in general terms – each person will react slightly differently to a given stone. The ideal stone for one person may not have any effect on another. Intuition lets the crystal worker choose the most appropriate stone for each case.

guided by instinct

Intuition is the sum of information that is received by the mind at levels of awareness that we do not usually access. Though an important factor in our everyday lives, intuitive choices usually go unnoticed. Often they are things we 'just do' without any conscious justification.

Paying attention to where our awareness moves – where the eyes may be resting, what the hands are doing, the sorts of thoughts in our mind, how the body is feeling – is important. It's also useful to take note of the actions we perform 'by mistake', like picking up a stone other than the one intended, or having a stone fall out of place time after time – all these are clues to intuitive knowledge. Intuition rarely operates at the level of spoken thoughts – it is necessary to have a quiet mind so that these subtle impressions are not drowned out by our usual mental chatter. This is why developing a regular meditation practice and removing our own stress is important. Taking time to experience calmness and clarity increases the likelihood of noticing what is really happening around us.

Regardless of how large or small your collection of stones, intuition will guide you to choose the most appropriate crystals for the work you are doing. When you go to select stones for a healing, notice those that first catch your eye. See if, when you pick up the stones, there is an instant of hesitation before you select a particular crystal.

USING INTUITION IN CRYSTAL HEALING

Noticing your instinctive actions, thoughts and feelings greatly increases the effectiveness of a crystal healing session. Be aware of hesitation before or after placing a stone – you may need to adjust the position. Notice if there is a feeling of rightness or completion when all the stones have been placed. If there is not, maybe another stone needs adding or some other change should be made.

Working with crystals teaches you to become aware of slight changes in your mental and physical state. When working with others, scan quickly across the patient's body to discover how they feel. Then note which crystal or group of stones comes immediately to mind. Practise your sensitivity all the time, not only with hand scans but also with visual scans. Remember that the individual energy field is greater than the physical body. When you quickly scan someone – does the energy feel balanced? Is there a sense of being top or base-heavy? Do you sense grey areas or energy hollows?

◁ **Intuition develops at its own pace. Regular work with crystals will ensure accuracy.**

▽ **Focus on maintaining a relaxed awareness rather than on any desired outcome.**

△ Regardless of how large or small your collection, intuition will guide you to choose the most appropriate crystals.

▽ Kyanite forms fan-like clusters or blades of thin crystal ideal for restoring energy balance.

deep blue crystals

Crystals of a deep blue colour will stimulate the latent abilities of subtle perception and intuitive skills. Stones with striations will speed the flow of information, as well as initiating levels of peacefulness through

▽ Indicolite is the blue-green variety of tourmaline ideal for working on the upper chakras and wherever a peaceful flow of energy is needed.

△ Sapphire can balance the higher faculties of the mind as well as reducing levels of stress.

which information can be recognized. Blue tourmaline, also known as indicolite, will energize and balance throat, brow and crown chakras in this way.

Kyanite (Al_2SiO_5) is a blue variety of the mineral disthene, which forms thin blade-like crystals. Kyanite is a very effective energy conduit that can balance most systems in the subtle anatomy. It can quickly create great stillness and tranquillity, which makes it ideal for meditation.

Corundum (Al_2O_3) can often be found in the same rock as kyanite. The presence of iron and titanium colours corundum blue, creating the stone we call sapphire. Forming hard, barrel-shaped or hexagonal crystals, sapphire will enhance the functions of the higher levels of consciousness, reduce tension and bring calm, especially to the crown and solar plexus chakras.

Amethyst and other violet stones

Violet stones have a natural affinity to the crown chakra just above the top of the head. This chakra relates to functions of the brain and mind, but most of all it is the master control centre for the whole chakra system. Violet stones combine the vibrations of practical, down-to-earth red energy with the energy of blue – the expansive, spacious, undefined flow of peace. Combining the two extremes allows violet stones to bring a state of balance wherever it is required, while having a special focus on the workings of the mind.

amethyst

A violet form of quartz, amethyst (SiO_2 + Fe) has always been prized as a beautiful gemstone and master healer. Coloured by

▷ Clusters and geodes of amethyst are ideal for placing in rooms as a focus for healing and peace.

AMETHYST HEALING NET

The amethyst net is an excellent method to explore the qualities of other crystals. It also aids any deep healing work and is especially useful for creating calm.

1 To enhance the effect of this net, lie on a yellow or violet cloth. Place eight amethyst crystals evenly spaced around the body, with one below the feet and one above the head. If you have amethyst points, place them so they face inwards. Have the stones you want to investigate close at hand.

2 When you are settled in the amethyst net, experiment by placing a stone at your brow chakra (or any other chakra point you want to try). Finish off all exploratory sessions holding a piece of black tourmaline to ground and centre.

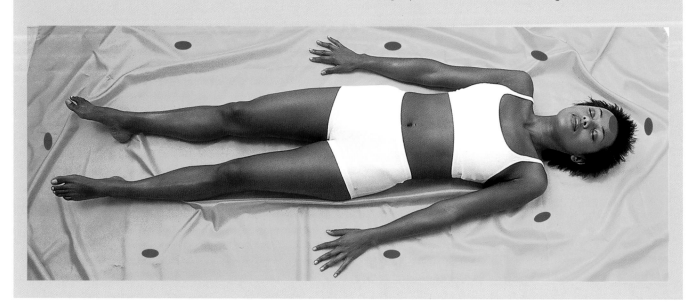

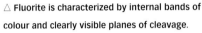

△ Fluorite is characterized by internal bands of colour and clearly visible planes of cleavage.

▽ First found in Japan, then South Africa, sugilite has become a popular stone for quality jewellery.

△ Violet stones help the mind to become more organized and orderly. This can aid where there is restlessness and difficulty sleeping.

▽ Dynamic rest and effortless action are the characteristic qualities that violet stones can bring to our lives.

iron, amethyst tends to form geodes of densely packed short crystals all pointing inwards towards the centre of the hollow. Colour varies from very dark, almost black, through purple to a delicate violet. Amethyst is calming and stabilizing to all areas, particularly the mind. It can be a useful stone to reduce restlessness, irritation and worry. Amethyst balances brow and crown chakras but can be used anywhere. Held or placed upon the forehead or above the crown, it is helpful for meditation. The combination of the grounding effects of red together with the expansive quality of blue allows amethyst to be an effective guide in the exploration of different states of being.

fluorite

A common mineral found in metamorphic rock, fluorite (CaF_2) has many uses in industry and is the main source of fluorine gas. Fluorite often has bands of different colours running through it, making it a popular decorative stone despite its softness and fragility. Common colours are blues and violets, green, yellow and clear. Fluorite is particularly useful as a balancer of brow and crown chakras – though it will help to integrate spiritual energies in a balanced way to any level of the body. It will encourage orderliness and structure and is especially helpful at improving levels of physical co-ordination and mental agility.

sugilite

A stone that was only discovered in the first half of the 20th century, sugilite (KNa_2 $(Fe^{2+},Mn^{2+},Al)_2Li_3Si_{12}O_{30}$) is another purple mineral that helps the co-ordination of the left and right hemispheres of the brain. The nervous system is balanced by this stone and it helps sensitive individuals who feel unable to keep up with the changes within society and technology. This inability can create confusion and alienation or can manifest as allergy problems. Sugilite helps integration with the everyday world, and can help prevent a withdrawal from it.

Multi-coloured stones – unlimited possibilities

Crystals displaying more than one colour can be especially useful for healing as they will introduce a mixture of colour energies simultaneously. A combination of red and green, for example, will be energizing but in a very organized way. Red-and-green stones, such as bloodstone or ruby in zoisite, can energize the heart chakra and calm the base chakra. A combination of complementary colours (red-green; blue-orange; violet-yellow; black-white) very effectively harmonizes and integrates related chakra energies and can help energy flow better throughout the whole system.

Azurite-malachite and chrysocolla display different shades of blue and green and therefore broadly balance the area of the throat and chest. Where one colour predominates, that will be the main energy involved, and other colours present will modify that primary focus. So a bloodstone will work mainly at a green level, lapis lazuli at a blue level and so on.

Some crystals display a whole rainbow spectrum of colours. These stones naturally attune to the very rarefied levels of energy above the crown chakra. They can also be used in the same way as white or clear stones, bringing in the whole potential of the spectrum of light. The colour in many of these multi-coloured stones is created by light refracting off their internal structures – microcrystals, fractures, inclusions and so on. Their appearance changes depending on how the light catches them, giving them an extra liveliness. Organic gems such as mother of pearl and abalone exemplify this very well.

opal

A member of the quartz family, opal ($SiO_2.nH_2O$) crystallizes in a slightly different form and has a high water content. Its watery quality and great range of colours aligns the stone naturally with the emotions and emotional balance. The opal will work with emotions in the area of its dominant colour.

Brown, black or dark blue opals will work well with the lower chakras and are particularly effective at releasing tensions in the reproductive system, being useful for painful periods and PMT. Fire opal, a bright orange colour, will energize and help recovery after emotional upset. Water opal, which is colourless with a sheen of rainbow colours, can help to stabilize mood swings and energize the subtle systems of the body.

◁ The high water content and microscopic structure of opal gives it a unique variety of rainbow colours and patterns.

△ Stones that combine red and green, such as ruby in zoisite, shown here, or bloodstone, help to enliven with their polarity of energy, both the heart and base chakras.

labradorite

A variety of feldspar, labradorite ($(Na,Ca)Al_{1-2}Si_{3-2}O_8$) looks dull grey until light hits the inclusions of magnetite crystals. The iridescence created is a vivid mix of peacock blues, yellows, oranges and greens. Like all stones with a vivid play of rainbow light, labradorite can inspire many different levels of energy and awareness. It brings energy into the body and works well with any of the chakras.

One of labradorite's most important characteristics is the ability to protect the auric field and prevent energy being drained by other people. This sort of energy drain is usually an unconscious process between people who are in a close relationship of some kind – family members or co-workers – where one person habitually absorbs the energy they need from the other. This leaves

△ The play of colour in labradorite helps to disperse enervating external energies to maintain personal energy integrity. A white variety is known as spectrolite or rainbow moonstone.

▽ Azurite-malachite is a good stone to calm the heart and emotions, restoring a sense of peace.

the second person feeling tired and drained, put-upon or overwhelmed. Wearing or carrying a piece of labradorite effectively prevents this excessive loss of energy. There may have to be some changes in the relationship as it comes to terms with a new balance of energies.

▽ Ametrine can be useful for easing worries, increasing creative imagination, restoring balance to the digestion and improving memory.

ametrine, azurite-malachite

Amethyst, when subjected to heat, turns golden yellow. Where the heating is uneven or localized there may be areas of yellow next to the original violet colour. This variation is known as ametrine. A combination of violet and yellow is ideal for balancing anxiety, fear and nervousness as it affects the solar plexus and brow chakras. Azurite is a deep blue copper mineral that gradually breaks down to form green malachite. Both are therefore often found together.

▽ Abalone shell is formed from layers of crystallized calcium carbonate, a substance known as nacre.

Crystal reference guide

These lists are best used as a reminder of the general areas of function rather than a rigid framework that must be adhered to at all times. The names of the crystals in the book are common throughout the English-speaking world. However variations do occur, due to the older names used in jewellery or mining that can sometimes be misleading. The chemical formula of a mineral remains a constant identification regardless of common names around the world and lists the constituent elements of a mineral and the relationship each atom has to the others. The formula for quartz, for example, is SiO_2, which indicates that every atom of silicon (Si) is bonded with two atoms of oxygen (O).

The colours listed here for each crystal are those most commonly found. Although colour is one of the best identifiers of a stone, most minerals can occur in most colours, and beginners can become confused, so other

Crystal	Chemical Formula	Colour
Amazonite	$KAlSi_3O_8$	Green, blue striated
Amber	$C_{10}H_{16}O+H_2S$	fossil resin Yellow, brown, green, red
Amethyst Quartz	SiO_2+Fe	Violet-purple
Apophyllite	$KCa_4Si_8O_{20}(F,OH).8H_2O$	Clear, green, grey, pink
Aquamarine	$Be_3Al_2Si_6O_{18}$	Blue
Azurite-malachite	$Cu_3(CO_3)2(OH)_2 + Cu_2CO_3(OH)_2$	Dark blue and green
Black Tourmaline (Schorl)	$Na(Mg,Fe,Li,Mn,Al)_3Al_6(BO_3)_3Si_6O_{18}(OH,F)_4$	Black
Bloodstone	SiO_2	Green with red spots
Blue Lace Agate	SiO_2	Blue, banded
Botswana Agate	SiO_2	White, grey banded
Calcite	$CaCO_3$	Colourless, all colours
Carnelian	SiO_2	Red-orange
Celestite	$SrSO_4$	Grey-blue, clear
Chrysocolla	$(Cu,Al)_2H_2Si_2O_5(OH)_4.nH_2O$	Green to blue
Citrine Quartz	SiO_2	Yellow-brown
Clear Quartz	SiO_2	Colourless
Corundum	Al_2O_3	All colours, white streak
Danburite	$CaB_2Si_2O_8$	Colourless
Diamond	C_4	Colourless, all colours
Emerald	$Be_3Al_2Si_6O_{18}$	Bright green
Fire Opal	$SiO_2.nH_2O$	Red, orange
Fluorite	CaF_2	All colours
Garnet	SiO_4 plus various metals	Red, brown, green
Gold	Au	Yellow, orange
Green Aventurine	SiO_2	with inclusions Green, blue
Haematite	Fe_2O_3	Metallic grey/black

identifying qualities such as crystal shape (crystal system) and hardness can be useful to know. Crystal system is not always easy to recognize because of the many variations within each system. However, certain characteristics of each system can really help identification. Mohs' Scale of Hardness is a scale of relative hardness. Minerals of 1 or 2 are extremely soft and easily scratched. A hardness of 3 to 5 can be dulled or scratched easily and so are rarely used in jewellery. Most gemstones range from a hardness of 6 (like moonstone) to 8 (like emerald). Stones harder than 8 are rare: corundum (ruby and sapphire) has a hardness of 9 and only diamond has a hardness of 10.

The influence each stone has with an individual's energy systems will depend on the state of health. However, the general qualities of each stone will suggest that they will work well in certain broad areas.

Crystal System	Hardness	Chakra	Subtle Body
Triclinic	6–6.5	Heart, throat	Mental, etheric
Amorphous	2	Solar plexus	Mental
Trigonal	7	Brow, crown	Emotional, mental, spiritual
Tetragonal	4.5–5	Heart, crown	
Hexagonal	7.5–8	Throat	Etheric, mental
Monoclinic	3.5–4	Throat, heart	Etheric, mental, astral
Trigonal	7–7.5	Base	Etheric, astral
Microcrystalline trigonal	7	Heart, base	Etheric
Trigonal	7	Throat	Emotional, mental
Trigonal	7	All	
Hexagonal	3	All	
Trigonal	7	Sacral	Etheric
Orthorhombic	3–3.5	Throat, crown	Soul
Monoclinic or orthorhombic	2–4	Heart, throat	Emotional, mental
Trigonal	7	Solar plexus	Causal
Trigonal	7	All	Etheric, emotional
Trigonal	9	Crown, solar plexus	
Orthorhombic	7	Crown	Spiritual
Cubic	10	Crown	Mental
Hexagonal	7.5–8	Heart	Astral, etheric, emotional
Amorphous	6	Base, solar plexus	
Cubic	4	Brow	Etheric
Cubic	6.5–7.5	Base	Etheric, astral
Cubic	2.5–3	Heart	Emotional, mental, spiritual
Trigonal	7	Heart	Etheric, mental, emotional
Trigonal	5–6	Sacral, solar plexus	Etheric

Indicolite	$Na(Mg,Fe,Li,Mn,Al)_3Al_6(BO_3)_3Si_6O_{18}(OH,F)_4$	Blue, blue-green
Iron Pyrites	FeS_2	Metallic yellow
Jade – Jadeite	$NaAlSi_2O_6$	Clear, rich green
Jade – Nephrite	$Ca_2(Mg,Fe)_5Si_8O_{22}(OH)_2$	Green
Jet	Organic carbon	Black, dark brown
Kunzite	$LiAlSi_2O_6$	Lilac, clear, green
Kyanite	Al_2SiO_5	Blue
Labradorite	$(Na,Ca)Al_{1-2}Si_{3-2}O_8$	Grey, green iridescent
Lapis Lazuli	$(Na,Ca)_8(Al.Si)_{12}O_{24}(S,SO_4)$	Deep blue with white and gold
Magnetite/Lodestone	Fe_3O_4	Black
Malachite	$Cu_2CO_3(OH)_2$	Greens with black
Milky Quartz	SiO_2	White
Moldavite	Rock silicates	Green
Moonstone	$KaSi_3O_8$	Pearly/cream
Moss Agate	SiO_2	Clear with green/brown inclusions
Obsidian	Igneous rock with inclusions	Black, grey, red-brown
Opal	$SiO_2.nH_2O$	Various
Red Coral	$CaCO_3$	Red, orange, pink
Red Jasper	SiO_2	Red
Rhodocrosite	$MnCO_3$	Pink, orange, cream
Rhodonite	$(Mn^{+2},Fe^{+2},Mg,Ca)SiO_3$	Pink with brown or black
Rose Quartz	SiO_2	Pink
Rubellite	$Na(Mg,Fe,Li,Mn,Al)_3Al_6(BO_3)Si_6O_{18}(OH,F)_4$	Pink, red
Ruby	Al_2O_3	Red
Rutilated Quartz	TiO_2 (in SiO_2)	Yellow-brown
Sapphire	Al_2O_3	Blue, violet-blue
Selenite	$CaSO_4.2H_2O$	Pearly
Smoky Quartz	SiO_2	Brown, black
Sodalite	$Na_4Al_3Si_3O_{12}Cl$	Blue with white veins
Spinel	$MgAl_2O_4$	Scarlet, pink
Sugilite	$KNa_2(Fe^{2+},Mn^{2+},Al)_2Li_3Si_{12}O_{30}$	Lilac, purple
Tektite	Rock, silicates	Brown, black
Topaz	$Al_2SiO_4(F,OH)_2$	All colours, clear
Turquoise	$CuAl_6(PO_4)_4(OH)_8.4H_2O$	Light blue–turquoise-green
Verdelite	$Na(Mg,Fe,Li,Mn,Al)_3Al_6(BO_3)_3Si_6O_{18}(OH,F)_4$	Green
Zircon	$ZrSiO_4$	Brown to clear

Trigonal	7.5	Throat, brow	All
Cubic	6.5	Solar plexus	Astral
Monoclinic	7	Heart	Astral, etheric, emotional
Monoclinic	6–6.5	Heart	Astral, etheric, emotional
Amorphous	2.5	Base	Etheric, emotional
Monoclinic	6.5–7.5	Heart, throat	Etheric
Triclinic	4–7	Throat	All
Triclinic	6–6.5	All	All
Cubic	5.5	Throat, brow	Etheric, mental
Cubic	5.5–6.5	All	All
Monoclinic	3.5–4	Heart	Etheric, emotional
Trigonal	7	All	Emotional
Amorphous	5	Heart, throat, brow, crown	All
Monoclinic	6–6.5	Sacral, solar plexus	Emotional
Trigonal	7	Heart	Emotional, mental
Amorphous	6	Base, sacral, crown	Mental
Amorphous	6	Sacral, solar plexus, crown	Emotional
Hexagonal or trigonal	3	Heart	Etheric
Trigonal	7	Base	Etheric
Trigonal	3.5–4.5	Base to heart	Emotional, mental, astral
Triclinic	5.5–6.5	Heart	Emotional
Trigonal	7	Heart, throat	Emotional, mental, astral
Trigonal	7–7.5	Sacral, heart	Emotional, astral
Trigonal	9	Heart	Mental, spiritual
Tetragonal	6–6.5	All	All
Trigonal	9	Solar plexus, heart, throat, crown	Emotional, mental
Monoclinic	2	Sacral, throat, crown	Emotional, soul
Trigonal	7	Base, sacral	Solar plexus
Cubic	5.5–6	Throat, brow	Emotional, mental
Cubic	8	Base	
Hexagonal	5.5–6.5	Crown	Astral, causal
Amorphous	5–5.5	Base, brow	Etheric, astral
Orthorhombic	8	Solar plexus	Etheric
Triclinic	5–6	Throat, all	All
Trigonal	7–7.5	Heart	All
Tetragonal	7.5	Base	

Suppliers

UK

Burhouse Ltd
Quarmby Mills
Tanyard Road
Oakes
Huddersfield HD3 4YP
Tel: +44(0)1484 655675
Email: sales@burhouse.com

Charlie's Rock Shop
Unit 14, 1929 Shop
18 Watermill Way
Merton Abbey Mills
London SW19 2RD
Tel: +44 (0)208 544 1207

Crystals
25 High Sreet
Glastonbury
Somerset BA6 9DP
Tel: +44(0)1458 835090
Website: www.crystalshop.co.uk

EarthWorks
43 Wessex Trade Centre
Poole
Bournemouth
Dorset BH12 3PG
Tel: +44(0)1202 717127
Email: earthworksuk@aol.com

Evolution
117 Fore Street
Exeter
Devon EX4 3JQ
Tel/Fax: +44(0)1392 410759

Simon & Sue Lilly
PO Box 6
Exminster
Exeter
Devon EX6 8YE
Tel/Fax: +44(0)1392 832005
Email: info@greenmanessences.com
Web: www.greenmanessences.com

USA

Crystal Magic
2978 West Hwy 89A
Sedona. AZ86336
Tel: (050) 282-1622

Multistone International
135 South Holliday St
Strasburg, VA 22657
Tel: (540) 465-8777
Web: www.multistoneintl.com

Rosley's Rocks and Gems
2153 N. Sheffield Ave
Chicago, IL 60614
(800) 844-1498
web: www.crystalmaster.com

AUSTRALIA

CK Minerals Pty Ltd
PO Box 6026
Vermont South VIC 3133
Tel: 61 3 9872 3886
Email: GYRIL@ckminerals.com.au

Living Energies
Shop B80 Chadstone Shopping Centre
Chadstone VIC 3148
Tel: 61 3 9568 2188
and
Shop 113 Wahringah Mall
Brookvale NSW 2100
Tel: 61 2 9907 1716

Crystal Living
Shop 270, Lower Level
Garden City Shopping Centre
Cnr. Logan and Kessels Rds
Upper Mount Gravatt QLD 4122
Tel: 61 7 3420 6700

Prosperous Stones
Shop B3 Bay Village
Hastings Street, Noosa QLD 4567
Tel: 61 7 5445 4622

Index